TALK TO THE MIRROR

TALK TO THE MIRROR

*Feel Great about Yourself
Each and Every Day*

Florine Mark

with Maria Scott

John Wiley & Sons, Inc.

Published by John Wiley & Sons, Inc., Hoboken, New Jersey
Published simultaneously in Canada

Design and production by Navta Associates, Inc.

For general information about our other products and services, please contact our Customer Care Department within the United States at (800) 762-2974, outside the United States at (317) 572-3993 or fax (317) 572-4002.

Wiley also publishes its books in a variety of electronic formats. Some content that appears in print may not be available in electronic books. For more information about Wiley products, visit our web site at www.wiley.com.

Library of Congress Cataloging-in-Publication Data:
Mark, Florine.
   Talk to the mirror : feel great about yourself each and every day / Florine Mark and Maria Scott.
      p.   cm.
   Includes bibliographical references and index.
   ISBN 0-471-63085-3
1. Self-actualization (Psychology) I. Scott, Maria. II. Title.
   BF637.S4M355 2004
   158.1—dc22   2004005659

Printed in the United States of America

10 9 8 7 6 5 4 3 2 1

CONTENTS

CONTENTS

CONTENTS

CONTENTS

CONTENTS

ACKNOWLEDGMENTS

I dedicate this book to my husband, Dr. Bill Ross, who always encouraged me to be the best that I can be, who laughed the first time he caught me talking to the mirror, but who eventually joined me in talking to the mirror every morning.

To my family, who have always been there for me and who always encourage me to live my dreams. To all of my friends, who have always wanted to know how I do it all. Without family and friends this book could never have been written.

To Sheryl Fellows, who has encouraged me to write this book since she started working for me.

To Maria Scott, who helped me put it all together.

And to Loretta Barrett, who found the perfect publisher for this book in John Wiley & Sons, as well as the perfect editor—Tom Miller.

PART I

Taking Care of Your Best Friend — You

*We have to learn to be our own best friends because we fall
too easily into the trap of being our own worst enemies.*
RODERICK THORP

*The world is a great mirror. It reflects back to you
what you are. If you are loving, if you are friendly,
if you're helpful, the world will prove loving and friendly
and helpful to you. The world is what you are.*
THOMAS DREIER

I'VE GOT A PRETTY GOOD IDEA what you're thinking. You've opened this book wondering if this is the one. You know, whether it's your first motivational book or your hundred and first, you're probably asking, "Is Florine Mark going to be the one who can turn my life around?" And I can answer you with one simple word: nope.

That's right, I admit it—I can't fix your life. And diet experts or fitness gurus or any others, for that matter, who say they can are kidding themselves and kidding you. Well, maybe that's not quite true. There is one expert who can fix your life and I'm here to introduce you. Go get a mirror. No, I'm serious, go get a mirror. This is not a figurative request. Put this book down and go take a long look in the mirror. Then come back. I'll wait.

I want you to describe the person you just saw. I've listened to enough answers from people—particularly women—over the years that I can give you a pretty good sampling of what most of you are thinking when you take that look in the mirror: "She's fat." "She's stupid." "She's weak." "She's hopeless." I've heard all these answers many times.

Now, take a moment and think about your best friend. I hope you have one. If you don't have someone you consider a best friend, think about a good friend from your past or imagine someone you'd want for a friend. How do you treat that friend? If she put on weight, would you say, "You're fat"? If she made a mistake, would you blurt out, "You're stupid"? If she made a bad choice, would you hit her with, "You can't get anything right. You're weak and hopeless"? Of course not. It would never occur to you to treat a friend like that. First of all, she probably wouldn't be your friend for very long, and second, it's just plain abusive. In fact, we tend to focus on our friends' good qualities. Sure, we encourage them to change facets of their lives that aren't working, but we accept their imperfections. We don't see their flaws as devaluing them and we certainly don't beat them up. Right?

Yet if you were thinking any of the nasty thoughts I mentioned when you looked in the mirror, you are abusing your best friend. I'm talking about your friend in the mirror. Think about it: she will always listen to what you have to say. She'll never tire of the conversation. She definitely won't walk out on you. *And you're beating the living daylights out of her!*

This first part is all about how you can learn to care for—and take care of—your very best ally: you! Why is that so important? Because it's the first essential step in getting more joy out of life each and every day. Many women think that if they could just lose weight, get a boyfriend, land that dream job—whatever—then they will be able to love themselves. That's simply not true. Love—real love—is unconditional. Sure, you might think your best friend would look better if she weighed less, but it doesn't stop you from loving her, right? Well, the same has to be true about your feelings toward yourself.

Since I'm going to be asking you some very personal questions, I think it's only fair that I get personal, too. The first chapter in this section will give you an honest look at my life, including how I learned to like the woman I see in the mirror.

I realize that you and I have just met, so you may wonder about my qualifications for writing about self-acceptance. I am the CEO of a profitable business that is renowned for successful weight loss. I was recently voted one of the top thirty entrepreneurs in the world. If you look at my picture on the dust jacket, you'll see a confident woman who's in pretty good shape. In short, you might think Florine Mark has everything—how hard can it be to like the person in her mirror?

There are two things you should know. First, my life was not always like this. Before I made friends with myself, well, there is no other way to say it . . . I was fat and poor. A mirror was the last place I wanted to look. And when I did look, I didn't have nice things to say about the person looking back. Second, despite the success I've enjoyed, I still have to deal with struggle, disappointment, and frustration like everyone else. And when I'm feeling stressed, my first impulse is still to eat my way through it. That's my negative coping mechanism—for some people it's biting their nails or drinking too much alcohol or spending money they don't have. For me, it's overeating. I talk to the mirror to manage those impulses and to overcome life's down times. It's a strategy that's been working for me for decades.

1

My Story

Life isn't about finding yourself—it's about creating *yourself.*
GEORGE BERNARD SHAW

*To be successful, the first thing you have to do is decide
what you want. The second thing you have to do is
decide what you're willing to give up to get it.*
FLORINE MARK

I

T'S EASY TO RECALL the very best thing about my growing-up years: home. My family gave me a lot of love, in part because they were very loving people, but also because there were so many of them! You see, "home" included two grandparents, my mother and father, six aunts and uncles, and two sisters. We were poor, although I never thought of it that way. The women in my family worked hard to create a nurturing environment for us with lots of warmth, laughter, and comfort food.

My sister Sondra contracted polio when we were very young, and back then there was no Blue Cross/Blue Shield, no HMOs, no health insurance, *period*. My father was a college graduate, but the living he made parking cars on a rented lot just wasn't enough. My entire family worked to make ends meet, and I was no exception. I had my first job by the time I was eleven, selling doughnuts.

School was even tougher. Remember those thin pretty girls—every school has them—the ones just born to be prom queens? Well, I wasn't one of them. I wanted to be—oh, how I wanted to be—but in a world where acceptance often depends on good looks, I didn't measure up. I was overweight. In my mind, I certainly wasn't pretty. I was a vulnerable girl brimming with tension and envy. And I had good reason to be tense. A malicious boy (who I guess had his own problems) started calling me Fat Flo and the name stuck. I hated it. And I responded by going home and eating for comfort. Those were the roots of my destructive eating cycle.

During the summer months, kids my age went swimming, and of course that was the last place I wanted to go. Putting on a bathing suit meant showing the world my fat thighs. So instead I went to summer school. It was a safe, structured environment where I felt equal with everyone else. I loved learning, and the extra effort enabled me to skip two grades. As a result, I graduated high school at sixteen. Two months later, I married a college student who was a very nice guy. In fact, he's still a very nice guy, but we just weren't right for each other. So why did we marry? Because most people we knew got married young. If a girl didn't get married right out of high school, she was considered an old maid. So I followed the crowd, and I used diet pills to lose fifty pounds so I could fit into my wedding dress. Even fifty pounds lighter, I wore a girdle that my aunt gave me for the occasion. It was just the way things were done in the fifties.

A year later our child was born, a beautiful baby girl. I tried hard to be a good wife and mother, even worked to help out while my husband completed his education. But before long I realized that my marriage had been a mistake. He was a good person, but no matter how hard I tried, I could not visualize us spending the rest of our lives together. So I did what was practically unthinkable at that time. I asked my husband for a divorce.

We'd relocated to Texas and, being new parents, hadn't had time to make new friends, so I didn't foresee a lot of social backlash. But there *was* backlash, and from a source I'd never considered.

My mother hadn't wanted me to marry my husband. She saw all the things that at sixteen I didn't see. Mostly, she saw that I was entering marriage thinking that he would make me happy. I saw marriage in terms of what *he* would do for *me*. Of course, my mother knew that viewing marriage in those terms was a prescription for misery. When I told her that she'd been right all along and that I was ending the marriage, I expected that she'd be satisfied with my admission that I should have listened to her. Instead, she told me I couldn't get a divorce. When I told her I realized I'd made a mistake and that neither he nor I should spend our lives regretting it, I couldn't understand her response: "But what will my friends say?"

I was speechless. It had never occurred to me that my mother's friends could be involved, that social backlash could be an issue for anyone but my husband or me. And while I was trying to absorb that, my mother said something that shocked me even more: "You're going to kill your father with the scandal." My father was in perfect health at the time.

It was a terrible time. I struggled to balance the sense of responsibility to my family that I'd been raised with (and that I feel to this day) with staying in a marriage that I knew could not work. In the end, I went through with the divorce. It was really the only choice I could make. I knew that any scandal or social backlash would pass but that an unhappy marriage was a life sentence for both of us.

I'd like to say that I was at peace the minute I made the decision, but that wouldn't be true. Divorce, even when you want it, is a miserable experience. My husband found someone else soon after we separated. He married her the day our divorce became final, and I sat on a park bench all day, feeding the ducks and crying. Sure, I knew we weren't right for each other, but to be replaced so quickly, so *easily*, was a terrible blow. Finally there were no more tears left and nothing to do but turn to the future.

I took my sweet baby girl and went back to my parents'. I continued to work, but I wasn't comfortable living at home. I responded to the stress in the same way I always had—I ate my way through it. Still, it wasn't long before I found one of the few ways out for a woman in the sixties: I married a second time.

My second husband was the strong, silent type. He had no highs or lows—he was as steady as a rock. It was all very romantic, but we had little in common except for our children. Having children to love had always been important to me, and soon I had five—and all the responsibility that came with them.

My husband was busy building a career. At the same time, my weight was always going up and down. I was either fasting or feasting. I used the only weight-loss methods I knew: diet pills and a seemingly endless list of crazy diets. All protein; eggs and grapefruit; cottage cheese; cabbage soup; even an all-ice-cream diet—you name it and I tried to live on it. And I have to say that some of them worked—for about a minute. I lost and gained the same fifty pounds time after time. And there I was, with fifty pounds to lose *again*. My children were starting school and I needed to go back to work. I wanted to get a job, but I had no college degree and little professional experience. Who was going to hire an overweight housewife? So, as usual, I reached for the diet pills, but with far from the usual results.

I was rushed to the hospital. I'd taken only one pill, but the doctor said I'd had an allergic reaction. My body had finally rebelled against all the amphetamines I'd been using. The doctor's warning was very clear: "If you ever take another one, I won't be responsible for your life." At this point, my problems seemed almost insurmountable. I needed to take control of my life both physically and professionally, but I had no idea where to turn.

I read about a new diet that you could only get in New York City: Weight Watchers. It was my moment of truth. I knew this was my last hope to lose weight, so I flew to New York, determined to make Weight Watchers work for me. I met with Jean Nidetch, the founder of Weight Watchers. Rather than attending weekly meetings, I came to New York monthly and stayed for a week, attending three meetings a day for five days. I flew into New York once a month and lost ten pounds each month. When I'd lost forty pounds, Jean suggested I buy a franchise and start Weight Watchers in Detroit. That day my company was born.

Anyone who's been to Weight Watchers in recent years knows that our group leaders provide a strong support system. All our leaders have been on the program and have met their goal. They receive ongoing training and meeting guides to prepare them for the job. That's now. When I first started out in Detroit, all I had was the diet and the right to use the Weight Watchers name in a few counties. That's it. I had no business plan, no meeting plan, and, of course, I had no marketing experience. Where in the world was I going to start?

I started with common sense. Where could I advertise that I would be sure to find overweight people? The answer: I hung a poster in a candy store that said COME LOSE WEIGHT WITH WEIGHT WATCHERS.

I held my first Weight Watchers meeting in a school auditorium on Tuesday, July 12, 1966. I chose Tuesday using the most profound business logic—it was supposed to be a lucky day. The first night thirty people came, but, of course, that number included my five children, grandparents, aunts, uncles, and a few dieters.

I peeked out from the curtain and saw those people waiting expectantly, many familiar faces along with a few I'd never seen. And I had an anxiety attack and headed straight for the bathroom to try to pull myself together. There I was in the ladies' room with my head between my legs, gulping for air, praying that I wouldn't pass out. I'd never spoken in public before! What would I say? What if nothing came out, or worse, I said something stupid? What would they do?

I forced myself to put both hands on the sink and confront myself in the mirror. I said out loud, "Listen, kid, you've got to get hold of yourself." The General Patton approach didn't do a thing to ease my panic. Then I asked the mirror a question: "What's the worst that can happen?" I pondered that for a few minutes, wondering if I'd ever heard of anyone actually dying of fright—I hadn't. More likely, I thought, I could faint. If that happened, at least I wouldn't know until it was over. I actually saw a little smile in the mirror then and my death grip on the sink eased a bit. And then I had a realization that changed my life. These people hadn't come to boo me. There was no one in the audience waiting to taunt me with "Fat Flo." These people had come for help, and it was up to me to give that help. I took a deep breath, walked straight out to the audience, and said what I'd come to say.

I made it through the evening, but I wouldn't be who I am today if I hadn't faced that fear. I could have buckled and gone home beaten. Instead, I talked to the mirror and it gave me just the push I needed. It was the beginning of a beautiful friendship between my mirror and me.

The next week sixty people came to the auditorium, and within a month, a hundred people were Weight Watchers. The business grew steadily from there. I'd bought franchises for a few counties. The territories covered the Detroit metropolitan area; Toledo, Ohio; and Essex County in Ontario, Canada.

In the beginning, I did it all. Besides being the business manager, I was the leader, the receptionist, the public relations director, the bathroom cleaner, and an active member. As I said, I lost forty pounds in four months, but it took me a year to lose the last ten. Many women find it difficult to lose the last of that excess weight, and I was no exception. The program was brutal then—three fish meals and one liver meal every week, no pizza; even watermelon was an "illegal" food. (Today there are no prohibited foods in Weight Watchers.)

Years of stress-induced eating proved a tough cycle to break. I loved my new business, but I was tackling the unknown every day and wondering if I was up to the challenge. My first instinct still was to put food in my mouth. But I kept right on talking to the mirror. Most of the time, I made the choice *not* to respond by eating. Sometimes I did eat but chose a comforting bowl of vegetable soup and a crusty roll instead of a hot fudge sundae. Sometimes I chose the hot fudge sundae. But I'd talk it over with the mirror, forgive myself, and get right back on track the next day. I finally took off those last ten pounds and kept them off.

As I continued talking to the mirror, I made some personal discoveries. Perhaps the most surprising was that although my mind had been focused on weight, weight, and only weight, my problem wasn't about weight. My problem was a lack of self-esteem and limited coping skills. Weight gain was merely a symptom. As I learned how to cope with life's ups and downs, I learned to like myself, and slowly, controlling my weight became less and less of an issue.

One of my happiest discoveries was that I was a great salesperson. Once I sold myself on an idea and shared it with other people, the passion and excitement I had for it was infectious. To this day, it's the very best thing I do. Equally remarkable is that I was able to recognize my own talent. I was able to look in the mirror and see something positive in the person looking back. I was changing inside and out, and in the process, I was on my way to realizing a dream.

My entire family became involved in the business. My mother answered the phone, and my aunts and uncles worked in the office. My father was a receptionist. My sister Sandy worked as a receptionist and a bookkeeper and, eventually, headed the financial department. Later, I gave Sandy half of my business. My sister Micki became the company's head trader. As soon as they were old enough, even my children became involved. They typed, cleaned bathrooms, and did other chores. When I couldn't get a sitter, they came along to watch and listen to me speak. If your own kids fall asleep while you're speaking, you know you're boring the audience.

This may sound like we were all one big, happy family and, for the most part, we were. My family was proud of the new business I was building and eager to help me in any way they could. I felt—and still feel—enormously lucky to have their support. But I think it's important for you to know that it wasn't all roses. As soon as I dared to dream, I had to decide what I was willing to give up to get it. That's the way it is for everyone, and most of the time, the bigger your dream, the bigger your sacrifice. I gave up time with my children.

To some extent, I had little choice. We had five children to support, a home, and all the other usual expenses; we really couldn't afford my being a stay-at-home mom. I needed to go back to work. Did I need to go out and build an international corporation? Of course not. And it didn't start out that way. But each success provided a new opportunity, and eventually the combined successes paved the path I took. I'll be the first to say that I took the trip not only willingly but *passionately.* Eventually, that path led me to financial freedom and enabled me to provide my family with opportunities that I couldn't have given them any other way. Plus, I've been able to help literally millions of people lead healthier, more fulfilling lives. If I had it to do over, I would.

It would have been easy for me to omit this part of my story. I realize that it will be controversial. Some women will agree with the course I took and others will disagree. I don't think all of my kids have forgiven me for not being at home. And if you're wondering whether I've ever felt guilty about not being there, of course I have. But those days are over and dwelling on guilt about choices isn't good for anyone. Guilt about the past can ruin the present unless you make amends where you can, know when you've done your best, and then put it away. So that's what I've done.

My children grew up and one day I came home to an empty house. The last of the kids had left for college and I was facing an empty nest. My husband had been off growing his business and I'd been off growing mine. We'd never had a lot in common, but now the gulf between us was enormous. We talked about it and mutually decided to end our marriage. The kids were living their own lives now and were not particularly surprised when we told them about our decision. I'd never felt so alone.

I dealt with the loneliness by throwing myself into my

work. I grew my business by buying franchises for more states. I went on all the Weight Watchers diet programs as they evolved. I can't sell a diet program that I don't believe in. One of the changes included physical activity as part of weight loss and maintenance. When I was fifty pounds heavier, I'd never been interested in sports, but I found myself becoming an enthusiast. That's how I came to be on the tennis court where I met Bill, my third husband. I glanced at the court next to where my girlfriend and I were playing and saw a man who immediately caught my eye. He was handsome, tall, very strong, and slim. My friend told me he was a doctor who practiced family medicine and he was single. She introduced us and that meeting changed my life.

This man was my friend, my husband, and my soul mate for twenty-two years. What made our marriage work? By the time I married him, I'd grown up enough to know who I was and what I needed. We had romance, but we also had commonality. We were both professionals and we both enjoyed family, art, golf, movies, opera, tennis, bridge, and travel. That wealth of common experience gave us a strong foundation. We built the rest from there.

Bill and I lived every day as an adventure. When it became clear last year that Bill's life was coming to an end, my husband continued to make the most he could of every moment. He lived every day he was alive, looking at it all as one last adventure we could share together. Bill made me promise to go on living life as an adventure after he was gone. So here I am. I miss Bill every day, but I remember to take joy in everything that is good in my life. There is still so much to be grateful for . . . and new adventures on the horizon.

I'm the CEO and president of The WW Group, the company that began with a poster in a candy store and grew into the largest franchise of Weight Watchers International. At its peak, The WW Group owned franchises in twelve states and three countries. More than 100,000 members attended our weight-loss meetings every week. Recently I sold about 75 percent of our franchises so that I could focus more of my attention on writing this book, touring as a public speaker, and spending time with my family. When we get together for a meal (which is as often as possible), it's quite a houseful. I make the most of today with my children—and now I have the added joy of grandchildren! Children everywhere, adults chasing after them, ten conversations going on at once—it's hard to imagine anything better. And still, good days and bad, I find myself back where it all started, facing myself, accepting myself, talking to the mirror.

I've always been fairly private about my personal life—I can't imagine anyone being completely comfortable seeing her life story in print. But I thought it was important that you know something about the road I've traveled up to now. Now it's time for you to turn the page and begin your own journey through the mirror to live the life you want.

QUESTIONNAIRE: First You Need a Map

When starting any journey, there is one thing you absolutely need to know before you take your very first step, and that is where you are right now. Just think about it. Wouldn't it help—even before you start—to know all the things that are working for you *and* all the things that are holding you back from feeling good about yourself? To that end, I've put together some questions to help you figure out where your life stands. It's an opportunity to ask yourself what you really like about your life and to think about the areas in your life you'd like to change. The result will be your very own walking map through the chapters ahead.

Remember, this is not a test . . . there are no right or wrong answers. No one is going to grade you on it. It's a survey, and everyone will answer differently, depending on her own circumstances. What's important is that you're really honest with your answers. Look into your soul and seek out your feelings. Tell it the way it is—not the way a parent, spouse, friend, or article in a magazine says it should be. After all, this book is about *how you feel* . . . and remember, anything you have to say is just between us.

In this survey, you're going to find questions about many different areas of your life. Take some quiet time to read through them and think about how satisfied you are with each area. "Quiet time" is really a very important part of what you're doing for yourself here. It's crucial that you read and answer these questions without distractions. They don't have to be answered all in one sitting either. You can take your time and think about them—there is no pressure here.

Next to each question is a scale from 1 to 5. Circle the number that best reflects how you feel about each question as it relates to your life.

A 1 means that you really want to make a positive change in your life. You feel that if this area were different, you'd feel a lot better about your life and about yourself. Don't feel bad if you get a lot of 1's. That's why we're here—to make the things in your life that aren't as good as you'd like them to be better.

A 2 indicates less dissatisfaction than a 1, but it does mean that you recognize a pretty strong need for change in this area.

A 3 is a middle-of-the-road response. If you choose a 3, things could be better in this area, or they could be worse.

A 4 means that, all in all, you're pretty happy with this area of your life. Sure, there is a little room for improvement, but basically you're content.

A 5 means that this area of your life is about as perfect as it can get. You've got it all going for you.

If you read a question that doesn't apply to you—for instance, if I ask how you feel about your relationships with your siblings and you're an only child—it's okay to just skip that question. Grab a pen, a pencil, or my favorite, a purple marker, and let's get started!

You on the Outside
How happy are you with . . .

1. Your weight?	1	2	3	4	5
2. Your fitness?	1	2	3	4	5
3. The way you dress?	1	2	3	4	5
4. Your hair color?	1	2	3	4	5
5. The style of your hair?	1	2	3	4	5
6. Your makeup?	1	2	3	4	5
7. Your skin?	1	2	3	4	5
8. Your teeth?	1	2	3	4	5
9. Your overall appearance?	1	2	3	4	5

You on the Inside
Do you feel that you . . .

10. Are worthy of love?	1	2	3	4	5
11. Deserve respect?	1	2	3	4	5
12. Have a good attitude? (On any given day, is your glass half full or half empty?)	1	2	3	4	5

13. Spend enough time laughing or just   1   2   3   4   5
    feeling happy on an average day?

14. Take enough time for yourself   1   2   3   4   5
    to relax/recharge your battery?

15. Are able to handle the daily   1   2   3   4   5
    stress in your life?

16. Can cope with unexpected   1   2   3   4   5
    problems?

17. Can face the things in life that   1   2   3   4   5
    scare you?

18. Try or learn new things as a   1   2   3   4   5
    regular part of your life?

19. Usually make smart choices?   1   2   3   4   5

20. Embrace change?   1   2   3   4   5

21. Ask for help when you need it?   1   2   3   4   5

22. Learn from your mistakes?   1   2   3   4   5

23. Live in the moment rather than   1   2   3   4   5
    dwell on the past or worry
    about the future?

24. Get things done on time—   1   2   3   4   5
    especially the things that you'd
    rather not be doing in the first
    place?

The Healthy You
How happy are you with . . .

25. The quality of your diet?   1   2   3   4   5

26. The amount of water you drink in an average day?　　1　2　3　4　5

27. The amount of energy you have?　　1　2　3　4　5

28. How much sleep you get on an average night?　　1　2　3　4　5

29. How much aerobic exercise you get?　　1　2　3　4　5

30. How much time you spend on lifting weights or other strength-building exercise?　　1　2　3　4　5

31. How often you see your doctor for regular exams and health screenings?　　1　2　3　4　5

Love, Marriage, Family, and You
How happy are you with . . .

32. Your love life?　　1　2　3　4　5

33. Your relationship with your parents?　　1　2　3　4　5

34. Your relationship with your siblings?　　1　2　3　4　5

35. Your relationship with your children or grandchildren?　　1　2　3　4　5

36. The amount of the time you spend with your family?　　1　2　3　4　5

37. The quality of the time you spend with your family?　　1　2　3　4　5

38. Your ability to cope with or resolve conflict between your family and you? 1 2 3 4 5

39. Your capacity for being supportive toward your family *and* your family's capacity for being supportive toward you? 1 2 3 4 5

40. Your ability to forgive a loved one who hurts you? 1 2 3 4 5

Friends and You
How happy are you with . . .

41. The number of friends you have? 1 2 3 4 5

42. The quality of your friendships? 1 2 3 4 5

43. Your ability to agree to disagree with friends? 1 2 3 4 5

44. Your ability to be as kind to yourself as you are to others—to be your own best friend? 1 2 3 4 5

45. Your ability to give and take constructive criticism? 1 2 3 4 5

46. The amount of time you spend socializing? 1 2 3 4 5

47. Your ability to say no to peer pressure? 1 2 3 4 5

48. How well you handle friends who want more time than you can give? 1 2 3 4 5

The Professional You
How happy are you with . . .

49. The work you do?   1 2 3 4 5

50. The supervisor you work for?   1 2 3 4 5

51. The company you work for?   1 2 3 4 5

52. Your coworkers?   1 2 3 4 5

53. Your staff?   1 2 3 4 5

54. The potential for growth in your current job?   1 2 3 4 5

55. Your work's effect on your personal life?   1 2 3 4 5

56. The amount of hours you spend on the job?   1 2 3 4 5

57. The length of your daily commute?   1 2 3 4 5

58. The amount of work you take home?   1 2 3 4 5

For Stay-at-Home Moms (or Dads!) Only
How happy are you with . . .

59. Working as a stay-at-home parent rather than working outside the home?   1 2 3 4 5

60. Your family's appreciation of the work you do at home?   1 2 3 4 5

61. The respect you receive from peers as a stay-at-home parent?   1 2 3 4 5

Your Personal Space and You
How happy are you with . . .

62. The part of the country you live in? 1 2 3 4 5

63. The environment (urban, rural, etc.) you live in? 1 2 3 4 5

64. The home (apartment, condominium, house, etc.) you live in? 1 2 3 4 5

65. The furnishings in your home? 1 2 3 4 5

66. The layout of your home? (Do you have private/personal space?) 1 2 3 4 5

The Keepin' It All Together You
How well do you . . .

67. Keep your home organized? 1 2 3 4 5

68. Keep your office/workspace organized? 1 2 3 4 5

69. Remember your appointments? 1 2 3 4 5

70. Arrive on time for your appointments? 1 2 3 4 5

71. Return borrowed items (books, videos, tools, etc.) on time? 1 2 3 4 5

72. Keep maintenance schedules (for your car, appliances, etc.)? 1 2 3 4 5

73. Pay bills on time? 1 2 3 4 5

74. Remember and plan for birthdays, anniversaries, etc. 1 2 3 4 5

75. Remember to write thank-you notes? 1 2 3 4 5

76. Return phone calls/e-mails in a timely manner?   1   2   3   4   5

77. Set priorities for your life?   1   2   3   4   5

The Fiscal You
How well do you . . .

78. Avoid credit-card debt?   1   2   3   4   5

79. Save for retirement?   1   2   3   4   5

80. Keep a separate savings account for emergencies?   1   2   3   4   5

81. Balance your checking account every month?   1   2   3   4   5

82. Provide for your family (life insurance, estate planning, etc.)?   1   2   3   4   5

83. Pay taxes on time?   1   2   3   4   5

84. Keep a budget?   1   2   3   4   5

The Future You
How happy are you with . . .

85. Your dreams for the future?   1   2   3   4   5

86. The plans you have to turn those dreams into reality?   1   2   3   4   5

87. Your willingness to make sacrifices to realize your dreams?   1   2   3   4   5

88. Having a timeline to realize those dreams?   1   2   3   4   5

89. Your ability to make lasting,   1 2 3 4 5
   positive changes for the future?

90. Your ability to live a full, happy   1 2 3 4 5
   life as you get older?

All done? Good. Now take a look at what you've circled. You are looking at your very own map that shows you everything that is working for you *and* everything that is holding you back. Most important, this map shows you the path you'll need to follow to achieve what you want—a life where you feel good about yourself each and every day.

It's important to know that this map is good for today, tomorrow, and probably next month. But over time, your map will change as your circumstances and priorities change. It's a good idea to take this survey at least twice a year to make sure that you're in touch with those changes. That way, you can continue to place your energies in the places that will make you feel the very best about yourself.

For the record, I have yet to meet anyone who circled all 1's (thank goodness) or all 5's (but I'm still working on it). We all have things that we can work on. But it's important to remember that no one can change everything at once, and anyone who tries is just setting herself up for a disappointment. You can use this exercise as a guide to help you set some priorities. Take a look at any 1's and 2's first. Increasing those scores is going to make you feel better about yourself right away. On the second leg of your journey, you can focus on increasing your 3's, and down the road, you might be able to fine-tune some of those 4's into perfect 5's. How? Read on—that's what this book is all about.

So now that you've got a clearer picture of the road that lies ahead, pack your mirror—you'll be needing it—and let's get moving. And remember, I'm with you all the way.

2

There's a Reason They Call It the Present

All of us tend to put off living. We are all dreaming of some magical rose garden over the horizon instead of enjoying the roses that are blooming outside our windows today.
—Dale Carnegie

There is one thing we can do, and the happiest people are those who do it to the limit of their ability. We can be completely present. We can be all here. We can . . . give all our attention to the opportunity before us.
—Mark Van Doren

You wake up in the morning, and your purse is magically filled with twenty-four hours of unmanufactured tissue of the universe of your life! It is yours. It is the most precious of possessions. No one can take it from you. And no one receives either more or less than you receive.
—Dr. Thomas Arnold Bennett

*If ever we are to enjoy life, now is the time, not
tomorrow or next year . . . Today should
always be our most wonderful day.*
—THOMAS DREIER

HAVE YOU NOTICED HOW the whole world seems to be set on fast-forward these days? We use every ounce of technology available, from e-mail to electronic organizers, to get as much done as humanly possible. Sometimes *more* than is humanly possible. The trouble is that we can get so caught up in the speed of it all that we often forget to stand back and ask ourselves: is this what I want my life to be?

And that's an important question. Because while we worry that time is running out to meet some deadline—completing a project at work, paying our bills, moving to a new home—time is running out on our lives.

The Gift of Today

It's scary to think about, but we're all on borrowed time. I think about how fast the last twenty years have gone and wonder if the next twenty will go as fast. Will they go faster? Do I have another twenty years? I don't know how many tomorrows I have left—no one does. All I know for certain is that I have right now.

So I begin each day by asking myself, *Florine, how do you want to spend the wonderful gift of this day?*

It's amazing how that one question can be such an eye-opener. Because when you answer that question, remembering that the day is a precious gift, two things start to become clear. The first is what's really important to you. The second is all the stuff that you've made important, but that really isn't so important after all.

Things That Get in Your Way

Before I started talking to the mirror, I wasted a lot of precious days dwelling on the past. Sometimes I dwelled in anger. I had an argument or someone wronged me, and I kept reliving it in my mind, holding a grudge. Now, if I have an argument or my feelings have been hurt, I ask myself, if this were my last day, would this be so important? The answer is almost always a resounding *no*. Gaining that perspective makes it easy for me—whether I was right or wrong—to be the first one to make peace. The sooner that balance is restored, the sooner we can both get back to making the most of the time we have on this earth.

Sometimes I wasted time feeling guilty. When my sister Sandy died suddenly, all I could think about was everything I should have, could have, or would have said or done differently. But the fact is that I can't change what's happened. It's the past—it's over. What I can change is how I'm going to live today.

It's not just the past that gets in the way of the present. We can also get distracted by the "what-ifs" of the future. What if I lose my job? What if my husband or boyfriend finds someone else? What if I can't pay my bills? What if? What if? Because the future is so uncertain, we can waste a tremendous amount of time fearing failure, rejection, illness or death, or being alone. The only way to keep those fears from taking the joy out of each day is to face them head on. Take control of what you can and make peace with what is beyond your control.

I'm afraid of roller coasters. That's an easy one—I don't ride them. I'm afraid of flying. In my business, I have to fly on a regular basis. That one's not so easy. But I finally asked myself, *Florine, do you really want to waste all these hours (that add up to days and weeks) worrying about flying?* Of course not. *Well, what are you going to do about it?* Well, I'm not going to give up my business—which is what I'd have to do to give up flying—so I guess I'm going to have to get better at managing this fear. And I did, in two ways. The first is that I keep busy. I never get on a plane without a riveting book to read or work that requires all my attention. When there is bad weather, my fear gets harder to manage, so I resort to the second method I use to control my fear. I take out my pocket mirror and silently ask myself the same question that I asked myself before my first public-speaking engagement: *what's the worst that can happen?* Well, the worst that can happen is that this plane will crash and I'll die. Then I remind myself that we all die and if it happens now, there is nothing I can do about it . . . and at least I'm doing the work I love. And I keep talking to myself until either I feel better or the plane lands (and then I *really* feel better).

Coping with Stress

Another thing that is guaranteed to take the joy out of the day is too much stress. We all have stress. Some stress is good for us—in the right amounts it can give us the push we need to reach our goals. The trick is knowing our stress limit and learning to cope with (or even avoid) negative stress. Exactly how much stress is too much or what creates negative stress is as individual as we are. For me, negative stress can be as simple as being late. I have a tendency to be late because I'm always trying to do so much. When I walk into a meeting or an appointment late, I feel so nervous and embarrassed. I apologize for my lateness and then spend the next five minutes wondering if the other people believe my excuse, if they've really accepted my apology, and if they're angry with me. I try to avoid this negative stress by scheduling my appointments a few minutes ahead of the actual time. If my meeting is at 3:15, I'll schedule it on my calendar for 3:05. I'd rather wait for five minutes than worry about being late. Being on time as much as possible is not only polite to others; it's important to my sense of well-being.

Another sure source of negative stress for me is too much news. It's important that we stay informed about current events, but it's a bad idea to spend too much time watching TV or listening to the radio that is all news, all the time. I once heard a therapist say that human beings are made to cope with the bad news that goes on in a village, but technology now brings us bad news from around the globe. She said that we're just not able to withstand those negative, traumatic messages for hours on end. I couldn't agree more. My advice is that instead of making dinner with news radio in the background, listen to some beautiful music. Instead of "unwinding" in front of the news on TV, watch a classic comedy, stroll around your garden, take a bubble bath, hold hands with your love, enjoy the miracle of your kids. You'll get more joy out of every day if you choose to focus on life's *good,* simple pleasures.

Perhaps my biggest source of negative stress is socializing. That often surprises people because in my work I socialize a lot. But if I know I'm attending a party in the evening, I could easily worry the day away about everything from what I'll say to how I'll look. Not long ago, I was planning a trip that included some parties. For days before the trip I agonized over what to pack. I'd choose one outfit only to decide it was too dark, too light, too bright, too something. Somehow I finally finished packing and left for the trip. I made it . . . but my luggage didn't. I ended up buying a pair of dress pants and three or four tops to go with them so I'd have enough to wear for a few days. All that agonizing, stress, and worry . . . and in the end, it was for nothing (and I had a great time!).

Afterward, I asked myself, *Florine, why did you get so worried about what to wear?* And the answer was, *If I look good, I think people will be more likely to accept me.* The truth is that no matter how successful you become, you will still want to be liked, accepted, part of the "in" crowd, even popular. And that's okay—unless you start living your life for the approval of others.

Do You Like Yourself?

You have to remember that this is your life, your present, your gift. A fashion magazine shouldn't decide what you wear. That's your decision and you should feel good about your choice. Instead of asking, Do *they* like me?, we need to ask ourselves, Do *I* like me?

Even though I'm not sitting next to you, I can hear more than a few of you answering, *No, I don't like me.* And honestly, we all have days that we feel that way. I know I do. But when I find those feelings lasting longer than a day, I know I'm wasting precious time, so I take action. You can, too.

Take a piece of paper and draw a line down the center of it. On the left side, write at the top "Things I Like about Me." Now list all the things you like about yourself. If you're really down on yourself, this may take some brainstorming at first but it gets easier. Here are some of my responses: I'm a loving person, I'm a hard worker, I have pretty eyes, I have thin ankles, I'm a great salesperson, I'm loyal to my friends and family, I volunteer for charitable causes, I have a great sense of humor, I try hard to be a good mother, daughter, and grandmother.

Now on the other side of the paper, put down "Things I Don't Like about Me *That I Can Change.*" Notice that I emphasized those last four words. I did that because dwelling on what you can't change is just wasting more precious time. (I always wanted to be at least five feet seven inches, but to my knowledge there is no Grow Watchers, so I have to learn to be happy being five feet five and a half inches.) Some of the things I listed here are: I have a quick temper (I like to think of it as being passionate!), I don't spend enough time with my girlfriends, I don't have a college degree.

You'll notice that there are more things that I like about myself than those that I don't like about myself. I have found this to be true of everyone I've ever asked to do this. You may also notice that you magnify the things that you don't like about yourself. I know that when I was fifty pounds heavier, I would have listed "being overweight" as something I didn't like about myself. Even though it was only one item, I magnified it until it overshadowed everything else.

Sometimes this exercise alone is enough to remind you that while no one is perfect, you are a good and worthwhile person. And when it's not enough, it tells you where to start to make your life (and yourself) better.

Focus on Things You Can Change

Choose something that you don't like about yourself *that you can change*. Then make a plan for change and make it happen! Don't fall into the trap of trying to make big changes too fast. For instance, if you wrote "being out of shape" as something you don't like about yourself, don't decide to make your first goal to walk five miles every day. That probably won't happen and then you'll just feel worse. Instead, take a walk a few times a week—even if it's just for fifteen minutes. Set small, achievable goals and you'll be surprised at how quickly you can change the things you don't like about yourself.

Make sure your plan provides for lasting change. That's the only kind that counts. If you feel you don't spend enough time with your family, one grand gesture won't make them or you feel any better. You've got to schedule time with them on a regular and ongoing basis.

Your Daily Agenda

I believe everyone should have a daily agenda. I don't mean everyone that's in business—I mean *everyone*. Businesspeople, stay-at-home moms, students, retirees, everyone. Agendas are a great way to make sure that you enjoy the gift of each day. Here's what an agenda can do for you.

Begin your day with a paper and pen to create your agenda. Ask yourself: What do I want to accomplish today? What do I *have* to do today? How can I make time for the things that I think are important? How can I make time for me?

Imagine you're a stay-at-home mom (maybe you are!). Your agenda might include: do laundry, clean bedrooms, pick up child from school and take him to soccer practice, visit parents, work on fund-raiser, get dinner, go to PTA meeting. Analyze your agenda. Ask yourself: How much of this agenda do I really have to do? What can I do less of or differently to work in my priorities, including making more time for me?

Of course, there are other items you could analyze. Why are you doing the fund-raiser? If it's an activity that gives you a sense of accomplishment or that you just enjoy doing, by all means, keep doing it! But if this is a situation where you offered a hand only to find that they took your arm, it's time to resign from the fund-raiser and give yourself a *fun* raiser. Treat yourself to a manicure, do some shopping or browsing, try some new makeup—do something that gives *you* pleasure and takes your mind off the "have-tos" of the day.

When someone says she needs something, it is normal and admirable to want to help. But when you're always the one helping, you end up running around like crazy—with no time to call your own. Where is the joy in that? You are *not* the fire department. Just because someone calls does not mean you should *leap* into action. When you take care of others at the cost of your own mental, emotional, and physical health, then the joy goes out of these caring actions and out of your own daily life. You'll end up being in a very tired, depressed rut—unable to handle the little glitches or curves that come along every day. And if it turned out to be your last day, is that how you'd want to spend it? You have to make a conscious effort to be in control of what you're doing, when you're doing it, why you're doing it, and perhaps most important, if you should be doing it all. This is *your* life—shouldn't some of it be about you?

There are other items on that agenda you can analyze. You might consider asking some of the other soccer moms to take turns driving. Sure, one afternoon you'll be driving four kids instead of one, but it buys you three afternoons of time for you. You can use the time to make changes from your "Things I Don't Like about Me *That I Can Change*" list. Other choices you might consider are taking a nature walk, chatting on the phone with a friend uninterrupted, relaxing with a cup of tea— whatever will recharge your personal battery. You'll find that putting that time into your own well-being really improves the way you view and approach your next task.

Most businesspeople have daily agendas. If you're a businessperson, your agenda might include projects to be completed, appointments to be kept, or meetings to organize. But do you actively schedule mental health breaks in your day? You should. Actually *write* into your schedule twenty minutes every day to read a book or to drink a cup of coffee with your feet propped up. Don't be surprised when someone walks past your desk or into your office and says, "Wow, it must be nice," or "I wish I had all that leisure time!" It is so easy to let that kind of comment take the joy out of the moment. But you've got to *know* in your heart that this is time you need—that you don't have to feel bad or guilty about it. If you feel that you have to answer, try saying, "Yes, scheduling these twenty minutes into my agenda gives me the energy to get everything else done. You should try it." Then go back to your book or your coffee. Either others will be okay with it or they won't. You're not responsible for how they feel. You're only responsible for how you feel.

If you have a love in your life, make sure your agenda includes him or her. I know a couple who both work and have two young children. Once a week, every week, they plan an evening that keeps them close. After work, they pick up the kids from day care, go home, have dinner together as a family, and play with their kids. As soon as they put the kids to bed, the wife takes a relaxing hot shower while the husband makes air-popped popcorn. Then he showers while she pours two glasses of wine and takes the drinks, along with the popcorn, up to their bedroom. They climb into bed—both with wet heads—drink their wine, eat their popcorn, and talk about their week. The conversation has thoughtful times and laughing times, but it's always *their* time. Then they turn out the lights and snuggle in for the night. It's a lighthearted evening that recharges their batteries. Are there other things they could be doing? With a family of four, is there always laundry? Is there extra work from the office that they could each be doing? Does the house need to be tidied up? Of course—and those things will still be there tomorrow. But if you don't schedule joy time, all the work—all the "have-tos"—crowds out the joy. And who wants a life like that? Not me!

I try to write my agenda every day no matter where I am or what I'm doing. Recently I had a wedding at my house. Seven guests stayed with me from Thursday to Monday. All day, every day, there were guests who wanted me to spend time with them. While I realized that it was up to me to make my guests comfortable, I also realized it was up to me to set boundaries for my well-being. Every day I scheduled quiet time alone for a half hour. The very first day, I said to my guests, "Excuse me—I need a half hour alone in my room to regroup." Every day I'd take that time to look out the window or read or watch TV. I felt completely refreshed by the time I came out. Were my guests offended? No! I'd come out and find one of them playing the piano, a few chatting in the kitchen over some fruit, others watching a movie. And you know what? They started scheduling their own alone time. It made the time together more relaxed and pleasant for everyone.

There are so many ways to get more joy out of every day. But to make room for that joy, you may have to face fears, learn to reduce stress, change things you don't like about yourself, or reset your priorities. I'm not saying that this is easy; I *am* saying that I think it's worth it to live the life you want. After all, none of us can afford to waste time being unhappy with our lives or ourselves. Life is a gift that we open with every new day—that's why they call it the present. But none of us knows how many "presents" we've got left . . . so we've got to make this one count.

EXERCISE: Build a Life Pyramid

Here's another tool you can use to keep your priorities in plain sight. I call it the Life Pyramid. It works exactly like the Food Pyramid, where all the foods that you're supposed to eat the most of to be healthy—fruits and vegetables—are at the broad base on the bottom. The foods that you're supposed to eat the least of (fats) are at the small point at the top. All of the other foods fall somewhere in between.

To build your Life Pyramid, get a piece of paper ($8\frac{1}{2}$ by 11 is a good size) and draw a large pyramid. Draw three horizontal lines to make sections inside the pyramid. In the small top section, put all the things that you want to avoid most. For me, those things would include crying, losing my temper, and feeling guilty. The things that you would like to avoid when possible go in the next section. I might put scheduling too much work for one day, being late for appointments, and getting stressed about social situations. In the third section, write the things that you would like to do more of. For that section, I think of taking time to try new things (like learning to speak Italian!), spending more time with my girlfriends, and relaxing. In the broadest bottom section, write your very top priorities. For me, those are spending time with my family, giving to others, and laughing every day.

Now take your pyramid and hang it up somewhere in your daily work space—on your refrigerator, on a cabinet next to your desk, wherever you'll see it frequently. Your Life Pyramid will be a regular reminder to make time for the people and things that matter to you most *and* help you get your daily recommended amount of joy. Remember, like you, your life pyramid is a work-in-progress. You can update your pyramid any time your needs and priorities change.

Some Great Resources

Embracing the Present: Living an Awakened Life by Leonard Jacobson

How to Stop Worrying and Start Living by Dale Carnegie

The Power of Now: A Guide to Spiritual Enlightenment by Eckhart Tolle

Present Moment Awareness: A Simple, Step-by-Step Guide to Living in the Now by Shannon Duncan

There Is Only Now: A Simple Guide to Spiritual Awakening, Unconditional Love, Liberation and Transformation by Scott Morrison

A Year of Living Consciously: 365 Daily Inspirations for Creating a Life of Passion and Purpose by Gay Hendricks

3

WHERE DOES THE RIVER GO FOR A DRINK?

*The driver knows how much the ox can carry, and keeps
the ox from being overloaded. You know your way and
your state of mind. Do not carry too much.*
—ZEN SAYING

*You can bend over backward so far
that you fall flat on your face.*
—BEN H. BAGDIKIAN

*Unfortunately, many people do not consider fun
an important item on their daily agenda. For me,
that was always high priority in whatever I was doing.*
—GENERAL CHUCK YEAGER

IF FAMILY AND FRIENDS are at the center of your life, then we
have something in common. As much as I enjoy my business

success, it would be meaningless without the people I love to share it with. I'd do anything I could to help any of them. But like all things in life, it's important that we balance what we do for others with what we do for ourselves and what we allow others to do for us.

I recall when my five children were still at home. I'd get up early to get them off to school. Then I'd go to work and run the company, making decisions, answering questions, and solving problems. Before I knew it, it was time to go home and prepare dinner. After dinner, I'd leave the house again to teach a weight-loss class. By the time I got home at night, I felt tense and jittery and didn't even know why.

One Revitalizing Hour a Day

I kept having those feelings until I learned to schedule an hour a day to replenish and revitalize myself. It sounds easy on paper, but anyone with a family, a job, or both knows that it's not. My husband wanted my time, my children wanted my time, my staff wanted my time, but I learned that no matter what, I had to protect that hour for me.

I look at it this way. There are twenty-four hours in our day, and each day we wake up to them is a gift. We need to sleep an average of seven to eight hours. That means there are sixteen hours left. If I'm going to give fifteen hours to everyone else, I deserve one. You deserve an hour a day, too, but you have to take it—no one is going to offer it to you. If you start feeling guilty about it, head straight to the mirror for a pep talk. Take a good look at that stressed person in the mirror and remind yourself that this break is necessary for you *and* those you love.

When you're taking that break, remember to spend it doing something that you find relaxing. Don't do what you think you *should* do or what someone else thinks you should do—*do what you want to do.* Enjoy a guilty pleasure without the guilt. For me, that might mean sitting down with a cup of tea; dancing to my favorite music; swimming, walking, or doing any other exercise that helps me work out stress; or spending time with my grandchildren—not as a gift to them but because being with them is relaxing for me.

Every once in a while, my break includes a bar of chocolate—maybe even a big bar. That's fine . . . as long as it's every once in a while! Whatever you do to relax should also be good for you. Before I attended Weight Watchers and learned to talk to the mirror, I turned to food as a source of comfort instead of facing things I didn't like about my life. As a teenager, I'd work to make a little money for myself, spend it on ice cream, and then hide it in the back of the freezer until I could get time alone. Then I'd eat the entire carton in a single sitting. At the time, I'd have told you that eating like that was relaxing and comforting but in reality, I was hurting myself. I was a closet eater. While I was stuffing food in my mouth, I had a sense of fullness, but I did it to hide from the emptiness I was feeling. I never felt refreshed from those binges. The more I ate, the fatter I got and the worse I felt—so I ate more, trying to feel good, and just got fatter and felt worse—what a vicious cycle!

These days, people are always telling me that my energy level is amazing. I'm not Superwoman. I'm so energetic because I've learned what I have to do to take care of myself, which includes exercising, eating healthfully (especially getting five to nine servings of fruits and vegetables each day), taking that daily hour for me, and loving a lot. I've even been known to take more than an hour.

Every now and then, my sister Sandy and I used to take two hours off during a workday to go see a movie. We were allowed—we owned the company—but it still felt like we were doing something we shouldn't. That's what made it so fun—it was one of those guilty pleasures. Hey, don't underestimate them—guilty pleasures are one of the things that make life worth living. And they can lift our spirits long after they're over. My sister is gone now, but the memories of our stolen visits to the movies are still with me. They were good times and just recalling them is enough to replenish my spirit when I need it.

Sometimes, if I've had a really rough day, I may choose not to answer the phone in the evening. I use the answering machine to screen calls in case there is an emergency—if it's that important, they'll leave a message. I don't want to hurt people's feelings. It isn't that I don't want to talk to them. It's just that I don't want to talk to them *right now*. I cherish my friends and family—they fill my soul—but sometimes I just need to be *quiet*.

Of course, replenishing myself takes more than relaxation time. I make it a point to get a good night's sleep—eight hours almost every night. Then, when I wake up, I have my talk with the mirror, enjoy a good breakfast, exercise, and start the day feeling renewed and ready to take on the world.

Team Efforts and Asking for Help

There are more steps you can take to keep your energy flowing. Too many of us think we can or should be able to do everything ourselves when in reality, it's not practical or even possible. Take this book, for example. My writer helped me organize my thoughts and convey my messages, my agent helped me find the right publisher, John Wiley & Sons helped me produce the book itself, and my director of communications helped me market it. Yes, *Talk to the Mirror* is my book, but the overall project worked because I asked the right people for help.

If you don't surround yourself with the right people, or if you do, but don't ask for their help, you're never going to get what you need or accomplish what you want. Sure, every now and then someone will offer help, but most of the time it's up to you to ask or you're not going to get it. That goes for the big things (like looking for work because you're suddenly unemployed) and the little things (like asking your kids to set the table or put away groceries). We've got to achieve a balance between giving and asking for help. The singer Dinah Shore once said that "trouble is a part of life, and if you don't share it, you don't give the person who loves you a chance to love you enough."

When my friend Sharon's father passed away after an extended illness, she was not only grief-stricken but exhausted. Several friends were at her house, helping her mother and her prepare for the funeral. When one of them suggested that Sharon take a late-morning nap, she readily agreed that she needed it. Sharon had gone several days without sleep. Not long after she turned in, Sharon's husband woke her and asked her to get up to make their preschooler some lunch. Incredulous, she asked, "Why did you wake me? You know how to make a peanut butter sandwich, and if you don't, there are a half dozen women in this house who do." Her husband, a great guy, was genuinely confused by her irritation and said, "But honey, you're always the 'go-to-it' girl."

Was Sharon's husband depending on her too much? Absolutely. Was that all his fault? Absolutely not. Sharon set those rules . . . as a *rule,* she took care of everything for everyone at home. Sharon, a smart woman, figured out the problem then and there. She didn't get up, her husband made the sandwich, their preschooler had lunch, and—with lots of reinforcement over time—the "go-to-it girl" now goes-to-it a little less.

Learning how to ask people for help takes time. You've got to make them understand that you really need their help.

When they understand that you're truly in need, most of the time they'll be happy to help. As a result, they'll feel needed and valued, you'll feel more energetic, and your relationship will flourish.

But always remember to say thank you. Do something a little special for those around you. Rewards are the gifts of life that make us feel good about ourselves. We all need those "ahh" feelings we get when we know we're valued. Give rewards often and you'll probably get them just as often in return.

Know Your Limits

Besides taking time for yourself and asking for help, it is very important that you know your limits. There is a difference between making the most of opportunities that come your way and taking on so much that you end up on overload. I knew that I could raise five children and run a business. I also knew that going to college on top of those responsibilities was going to be too much for me. You have to make your choices based on what you want, how much you want it, and what you're willing to give up to get it. (For more on making choices, see chapter 7.)

My friend Marilyn once told me that she learned her limits the hard way. One morning about five years ago, Marilyn woke from a sound sleep hardly able to breathe. Her heart was pounding, she was bathed in sweat, and she was terrified beyond reason. After several agonizing minutes, she was finally able to breathe easier. It was the first such attack Marilyn had ever experienced, but it wasn't the last. The attacks not only became more frequent, but she developed more symptoms, including numbness in her fingers, high blood pressure, and muscle spasms. Her overall health began to suffer. After her doctor ruled out possible physical causes, he diagnosed the episodes as panic attacks and suggested that Marilyn seek counseling. Although she was uneasy about the idea of talking to a stranger, Marilyn was feeling desperate enough to give it a try.

Her counselor, Jon, asked Marilyn what was going on her life. She told him she was busy. Lately, many of her family members and friends had needed her support. Her father had suffered a severe stroke that left him wheelchair-bound and suffering from dementia. With her husband Ryan's support, Marilyn had moved back into her parents' home to help her mother care for her father. She brought their infant son with her. Ryan and she took turns making the hour-and-a-half commute to see each other several times a week. Not long after, her parents' business began to fail and Marilyn worked to get it back on track. To help with expenses, she also took on freelance work as a grant writer. Finally, two of her dearest friends were losing their husbands (both only in their forties) to cancer, and she tried hard to give them her support.

Jon listened carefully and then asked her a question that eventually changed Marilyn's approach to life: "Where does the river go for a drink?" When she said she didn't understand what he meant, Jon explained. "You're like a river, giving a drink to everyone who needs it and that's wonderful but . . . where do *you* go for a drink? Where do you go for help to replenish what you've given?" Marilyn's only answer was that there was never time. "*That's* why you're having panic attacks, he said. "You're simply running dry."

Actually, there was nothing simple about it. Marilyn—and her family—had to make some difficult changes so that she could get the rest and replenishment she needed on a regular basis. Besides taking some time for herself, Marilyn had to learn to ask for help to deal with situations that had become overwhelming.

It didn't happen overnight, but when Marilyn was able to ask for help, and her family came to understand that she *needed* help, they were there for her. Her mother made the tough decision to admit Marilyn's father to a nursing home. Seeing her daughter suffer made her realize that neither Marilyn nor she was up to giving him the care he needed. Marilyn's mother, sister, and brother-in-law visited him every day to keep him company and make certain he was well cared for. It was a tremendous comfort to Marilyn knowing they were there. Ryan changed jobs to relocate with Marilyn while she continued to stabilize the family business and care for their son. Her friends visited often, sometimes taking her to lunch or even treating her to a manicure or a facial. The panic attacks lessened over time until eventually they vanished.

Besides learning to ask for help, there was one other skill that Marilyn could have learned earlier to keep her river from running dry: how to delegate responsibilities.

Delegate

The ability to delegate is a learned art. First, you have to learn what you can and can't delegate. If the task you're facing could actually be life-altering, maybe it's something you should do for yourself. If it's a task that you'll need to do only once, it may not be worth the time it takes to delegate (unless you are being snowed under by other responsibilities). But if it's a task that will have to be done more than once, it's almost always worth investing the time it takes to delegate.

Next, you have to learn who you can entrust with a delegated task. How do you know whom you can trust with the responsibility? That's the trick—you can never know for sure until you take the chance of trusting someone.

You also have to accept the fact that most tasks you delegate won't be done perfectly the first time. You have to give good direction, be patient with the person you've entrusted with the task, give constructive and specific feedback about what can be done better in the future, and show your appreciation for his or her efforts.

There is one more key to successful delegation: you have to actually let the person do the task. This is not as easy as it may sound. It is difficult to give up control of a task to someone else. In the back of our minds, we tend to think that we could do it faster, better, smarter. That is a dangerous pitfall. When we have that mind-set, we tend to take on too much *and* it makes the people who are helping us feel frustrated and resentful. Before long, they won't want to help anymore. There is almost always more than one right way to perform a task. If you're going to delegate it, then you've also got to let people go do it, and that includes letting them do it their own way. The end result—and having the support of people who *want* to help you—is what really matters.

Now that you know some of my strategies for avoiding overload, why don't you take a closer look at how you've been handling your own busy life with the self-test below.

SELF-TEST: Is Your Energy Flowing or
Are You Running on Empty?

Choose the answer that best reflects you and your life for each of the following twelve questions.

1. How do you prefer to work?
   a. Alone.
   b. As a member of a team.

2. How often do you see or talk to your friends?
   a. At least once a week or more.
   b. Rarely; I live far away from my friends and/or don't have time to get together with them.
   c. At least once a month.
   d. I have a lot of acquaintances but really no close friends.

3. Do you have a difficult time saying no even when you know you don't have time or have already done your share?
   a. No; I know when to say no.
   b. Yes; I just can't say no.

4. If you were given three extra hours in a day, what would you do with them?
   a. Catch up on work or my to-do list.
   b. Go play tennis, golf, or some other sport I enjoy.
   c. Sleep.
   d. Curl up with a good book or watch a movie.

5. Do you have difficulty delegating responsibilities to others at work and/or at home?
   a. Yes; I know that I'd better do it myself if I want it done right.
   b. No; I know I can't do it all, so I ask for help and gratefully accept it.

6. How is your health?
   a. Great!
   b. No major complaints, but I feel run-down and am prone to headaches and/or colds.
   c. I suffer from chronic pain or illness.

7. Do you take everything too seriously? Do you miss the humor when everyone else is laughing?
   a. Yes; I'm pretty serious by nature.
   b. Yes; I really don't have time for all that.
   c. No; nothing brightens my day like a good laugh.

8. Overall, how is the giving in your relationships?
   a. Fairly equal most of the time.
   b. I tend to give more than I get.

9. How do you feel at the end of most days?
   a. Tired but unable to relax.
   b. Like I got a lot accomplished and thinking about what I've got to do tomorrow.
   c. Tired or sleepy and glad to be spending the evening relaxing.

10. When you're feeling overwhelmed, what are you most likely to do?
    a. Talk to a friend or family member and ask for help.
    b. Ignore it—this, too, shall pass.
    c. Channel all that anxiety into getting more done.
    d. Talk to the mirror to destress, prioritize, and eliminate unnecessary tasks.

11. How often do you take time for hobbies or your personal interests?
    a. I try to fit them in whenever time permits.
    b. What hobbies? What personal interests?
    c. Often—at least a couple of times a week.

12. On average, how much do you sleep each night?
    a. Eight hours, give or take a half hour.
    b. Nine hours or more.
    c. Six hours or less.

Scoring the Answers

1. a = 1: You may have a problem asking for help or delegating responsibilities.

   b = 5: Dividing the work can help you preserve your energy, and the satisfaction that comes with teamwork can energize you.

2. a = 5: Spending time with friends on a regular basis can energize your mind and spirit.

   b or d = 1: Whether it's a problem of distance, time, or quality, if you don't spend time regularly with true friends, you're not getting the benefits.

   c = 3: This is better than not seeing them at all, but it's a little sparse.

3. a = 5: You protect your energy reserves if they're running low.

   b = 1: You are probably overloading yourself.

4. a = 1: It's time to give it a rest. The to-do list will still be there tomorrow.

   b = 5: If you enjoy physical activity, you can get the double benefit of relaxation and better health.

   c = 1: If you chose "sleep," you're probably not getting enough, or you want to sleep all the time (this can be a sign of depression).

   d = 5: You're giving yourself permission to relax.

5. a = 1: You need to revisit this chapter's section on learning to delegate.

   b = 5: Delegation is another way of dividing the work to preserve your energy.

6. a = 5: The better your health, the more energy you're likely to have.

   b = 3: Frequent headaches and/or colds (or other infections) can mean that you are run-down. Your body is trying to tell you to take better care of yourself with diet, exercise, and relaxation.

c = 1: Ongoing pain or illness can sap your physical and emotional energy like nothing else. Make becoming as healthy as possible a top priority.

7. a = 3: Even if you're serious by nature, you can learn to lighten up. You don't have to become a stand-up comedian. Just adding some smiles and chuckles to your day will make you feel better.

   b = 1: If you don't have time to laugh, you really are on overload (see chapter 12).

   c = 5: Daily laughter lightens your stress and lifts your spirit.

8. a = 5: Relationships are rarely fifty-fifty, but that's healthy as long as the give and take generally balances out.

   b = 1: If you're always giving of yourself without getting something in return, you're bound to run dry.

9. a = 1: You need to learn to de-stress (see chapter 9).

   b = 3: It's important to learn to leave your work at the door.

   c = 5: As you rest and relax, you're recharging your energy.

10. a or d = 5: It takes a lot of energy to hold in your worries. Talk them out and you'll feel your energy return.

    b = 1: While "this too shall pass" is one of my favorite sayings (because it lifts my spirits and it's true!), that doesn't mean you should ignore what's overwhelming you. If you do, you'll just continue to be overwhelmed. Talk to a friend, talk to the mirror, or write it out on paper to prioritize and eliminate unnecessary tasks.

    c = 1: This is just another way of ignoring what's overwhelming you instead of resolving it.

11. a = 3: There is rarely time for hobbies and personal interests unless we make them a priority.

    b = 1: Hobbies are a great way to de-stress and reenergize.

c = 5: You're reenergizing on a regular basis. That's great!

12. a = 5: You're getting the recommended amount of sleep for optimal energy.

b or c = 1: Sleep is another activity that requires balance. Too little or too much isn't good for us.

Evaluating Your Score

12–39 You are suffering a major drought! If you don't start making time to relax, take better care of yourself, ask for help, and delegate tasks, you could find yourself in an energy (and health) crisis!

40–49 You're maintaining, but your energies are a little depleted. Take a look at the individual questions to see where you could have scored higher and implement those options as strategies to fill up on energy, health, and a sense of well-being.

50–60 You are doing what it takes to restock and restore the energy you're using on a regular basis. Congratulations!

Some Great Resources

Chicken Soup for the Soul by Jack Canfield

The Little Book of Letting Go: A Revolutionary 30-Day Program to Cleanse Your Mind, Lift Your Spirit and Replenish Your Soul by Hugh Prather

Mom Management: Managing Mom Before Everybody Else by Tracy Lyn Moland

The Self-Nourishment Companion: 52 Inspiring Ways to Take Care of Yourself by Matthew McKay

20-Minute Retreats: Revive Your Spirit in Just Minutes a Day with Simple Self-Led Practices by Rachel Harris

The Woman's Comfort Book: A Self-Nurturing Guide for Restoring Balance in Your Life by Jennifer Louden

4

The Golden Rule Gets a Makeover

Self-love is not opposed to the love of other people.
You cannot really love yourself and do yourself a
favor without doing other people a favor and vice versa.
—Dr. Karl Menninger

The smartest thing I ever said was "Help me!"
—Anonymous

If you must love your neighbor as yourself,
it is at least as fair to love yourself as your neighbor.
—Nicolas de Chamfort

Be patient with everyone but above all with yourself.
—St. Francis de Salles

Although this is my first time writing a self-help book, I've been a self-help book reader for years. I'm always on the lookout for new advice that I can use to make my life better and happier. And often, I find that some of the best new advice is really wisdom that has been around for a long time. Maybe it's been updated or expanded for our lives today. Take the example of the saying "An apple a day keeps the doctor away." That is some of the oldest advice for healthy living that I know, and it still holds true. Today we know why that apple kept the doctor away. Apples are full of vitamins, minerals, and fiber that your body needs. And the pectin and antioxidants in apples may even prevent some cancers. We've taken that knowledge and expanded the old saying about apples into even better advice for healthy living: eat five to nine serving of fruits and vegetables every day. Okay, maybe it's not as catchy as "An apple a day," but the idea behind it is the same . . . and even better.

Another classic saying for living a better life is the Golden Rule: "Do unto others as you would have them do unto you." Or, in more modern terms, treat everyone the same way that you want to be treated. It's a simple philosophy . . . but if everyone followed it, can you imagine how much kinder and brighter the world would be?

The Golden Triangle

But, just like "An apple a day," I think we can also improve this classic piece of advice if we expand it for life today. The Golden Rule is a great foundation, but I think it should be more like the Golden Triangle. The second side should say: it would be wonderful if everyone treated you as well as you treat them. It is so important to give *and receive* kindness, recognition, and love every day. And we absolutely need a third side to complete our triangle that says: treat yourself as well as you treat everyone else, or forgive *yourself* in the same way that you forgive other people.

Let's take a closer look, starting with the bottom of the triangle: "Do unto others as you would have them do unto you." If we're saying or doing things to others that would be hurtful if they said or did them to us, then we shouldn't be saying them or doing them. Sometimes it's difficult not to say what's on our minds—especially when we're angry—but usually, it serves everyone better when we hold back from saying things in the heat of the moment.

Isn't it amazing how even one sentence—a few spoken words—can affect a person's whole day . . . in a good way or a bad way? Isn't it amazing how much power each of us holds over the feelings of those around us? And if what we say can have that much impact on others, how much kinder would it be to choose words that make them smile . . . words that make them feel good? Wouldn't we want someone else to do the same for us? The little things we say to our spouses, family, friends, and coworkers can mean so much to them. Our words can make them feel happy or make them feel bad.

Think back to the last time someone hurt your feelings. Maybe you were able to shake it off and go on about your day. Or more likely, you spent at least part of that day feeling bad. Plus, I'm willing to bet that the person who hurt your feelings— if she realized she was being hurtful—spent some time during her day feeling pretty bad herself. She may wish she could take back what she said or even wonder *why* she said it. If we can keep that in mind—the power our words can have—and use the Golden Rule, we can make their days and our days so much better.

Once, during a phone call to my son, he told me something that he had chosen to do—something I didn't particularly like. I was in a bad mood to begin with, and I found myself telling him exactly how I felt about it. My angry words made him feel hurt and angry, and soon our conversation became pretty heated. By the time we hung up, we both felt miserable. It wasn't long before I was asking myself why I said the things I'd said. So I called him back and apologized. I told him that it wasn't my place to judge the choices he was making about his own life, that he had to do what he felt was right for him. My son said that he was so glad that I called, that he felt bad that I was mad at him, and he forgave me right away. I told him how much I loved him and he told me that he loved me, too. When we hung up from that second conversation, both my son and I felt so much happier. It would have been better if I'd never said those angry words to begin with—and you can never *un*say them—but giving a heartfelt apology as soon as you can is the next best thing.

I had another family experience that shows how much happier the day can be when you *don't* say those angry words. I told my husband, Bill, I'd be working on my book all day and asked him not to call me unless it was an emergency. The phone rang and I was told that Oprah Winfrey was on the line. For just a second, I got really excited—my heart even started beating faster. But then my excitement turned into curiosity. I thought, Oprah and I have never met—who do I know that could have told Oprah Winfrey that I'm writing a book? I picked up the phone and it was Bill on the line, talking like Oprah to tease me. We had a good laugh, we said our I love yous, and hung up from the conversation feeling great. The outcome could have been very different. I could have gotten irritated and said, "I *told* you I was working—why did you bother me?" He would have felt bad, I would have felt mad, and we'd have both hung up feeling miserable. The way I responded was entirely *my* choice . . . and *my* responsibility. We can't always control what goes on around us, but we can control how we respond—and that can make all the difference in our attitude and feeling of well-being. Now that conversation is another happy memory of Bill's and my life together instead of a regret. The power of your words can make you—and those around you—feel good or bad. So be careful what you say. Save yourself from days spent wishing you'd said loving instead of hurtful things to those you around you.

Last week I stopped at the supermarket that I go to all the time and, for some reason, found long lines in every checkout aisle; a couple of the checkouts were closed, too. It had been a long day and I just wanted to get home. While I was waiting and feeling irritated that not all the lines were open, I noticed the cashier had a new haircut that looked terrific. She was also looking pretty frazzled, scanning items as fast as she could. Finally, it was my turn to check out. I had a choice. I could say something negative, pointing out the obvious—that the store was so busy, that the lines were too long, and that all the checkouts should be open. Instead, I said to her, "I see you got a new haircut. Wow, you look terrific!" Her face brightened into a smile, she stood up a little straighter, and said, "Thanks—I really like it, too." I glanced back over my shoulder on the way out, and you know what? She was still scanning items as fast as she could—and probably still feeling frazzled—but she was smiling while she did it. I knew how she felt from my own experience. Nothing brightens my day more than when someone gives me an unexpected compliment or notices a little extra effort I've made in my appearance or something I've accomplished. It was just one sentence—the Golden Rule at work— but it brightened her mood and made a hectic day a little easier for her. As I left the store, I found that I was no longer dwelling on the long lines or my tired feet. I was smiling, thinking about the smile on that cashier's face. Following the Golden Rule had brightened my day, too.

What about You?

This brings us to the second part of the Golden Triangle: it would be wonderful if everyone treated you as well as you treat them.

I think it's difficult for most of us to ask, What about me? We become so used to giving, so used to nurturing, that we feel uncomfortable about asking for the same treatment we so willingly give to others.

Sometimes it's actually easier to lash out at people rather than ask for those loving rewards. I can remember seeing a teen behaving very rudely to others. When I asked her why, she said that nobody paid any attention to her otherwise. In her mind, negative attention was better than none at all. I reminded her that being unkind may get attention, but it doesn't get rewards. And that's really what we all want and need. Those little rewards and compliments that we get from others are the sustenance of life. They keep us going when we're facing many of our life's challenges.

Being a martyr is another way some people try to get pats on the back. Martyrs do all the giving, while telling people how selfless they are the whole time they're doing it. Don't be a martyr. The truth is that martyrs never win. When I was growing up, I had a friend who also came from a big family like I did. She lived with her parents, two brothers, two sisters, and her grandmother. I can remember her grandmother always going around the house tidying up and complaining the whole time about what a mess everyone else made and how tiring all this cleaning was for her. She'd wonder out loud what the family would ever do if she stopped picking up after everyone. What she really wanted was for someone to tell her that they valued the work she did to keep the house looking neat. When she didn't get that recognition, she started making those comments, hoping to get the pat on the back she really deserved. Unfortunately, those comments made most of her family members feel annoyed and they ended up ignoring her even more. Being a martyr is definitely not the way to get loving recognition.

So how do you get people to act toward you in the same

loving way that you act toward them? Well, you have to ask them. You have to sit down with your loved ones and tell them how much you appreciate them and all the things they do, but that sometimes you need some recognition for the things you do, too. It's tough saying, What about me? But if you don't, who will? We all need those feel-good rewards, and asking for that kind word is worth it. Making a trial run at the mirror can help.

Look into the mirror and say, "I am a good person and I deserve to be appreciated for the hard work that I do." Then tell your friend in the mirror—you—all the great things about you and what you do for others. That list is so important . . . if you don't recognize your own worthy qualities and efforts, how can you feel confident about asking others to notice? Think about all the things you do to make things nicer or better at home, at the office, or by volunteering. It's just you and your mirror—don't hold back.

You might also want to try role-playing. Look into the mirror and pretend that you're talking to your family, your friends—whoever is not giving you the recognition you deserve—and say something like, "I work so hard at trying to make life good for us." Go ahead and list some examples. "I make fresh orange juice in the morning." "I drive you to your soccer games." Don't be shy about mentioning the things that you go out of your way to do. Then look your reflection squarely in the eye and pretend you're saying to your loved ones, "It would really help me if, once in a while, you guys could say thank you or let me know that you appreciate it." Say it out loud—get as comfortable as you can *saying* the words.

Then it's time to have the talk for real. Don't be mad or indignant or sullen. Just calmly say what you have to say. It's usually not that family and friends don't care. Often they just get so busy with their own lives that they don't realize they're not returning the loving treatment that you're giving them. Just have the courage to ask for the feel-good rewards you need—that's usually all it takes to get them. Soon, you'll be finding more smiles on your face more often and probably on their faces, too. Giving *and* receiving kinds words makes us all winners.

The 70/30 Rule

If it's not enough, you may want to try a concept that I've used successfully for years. It's called the 70/30 Rule, and it works with spouses, children, friends, bosses—everyone and anyone. I figure that if being around you makes me happy and I really enjoy our relationship at least 70 percent or 80 percent of the time, but 20 percent or 30 percent of the time I don't love all the things you do, I'm going to overlook that 20 percent or 30 percent. I'm going to concentrate on the 70 percent or 80 percent that I love. Ignoring the 20 percent or 30 percent is worth it to me to get the 70 percent or 80 percent that I love so much about the people in my life.

It's important to remember that 70/30 is just an average. There will be days when you love everything about a person— it's 100/0, a wonderful experience in every way. There may be a few days when only 20 percent or 30 percent of what he says or does is likable. Or he may be fine, but you're feeling overly sensitive. Bad days happen. If the average starts to slip to 60/40 or to 50/50 for any length of time, I start keeping my eye on that relationship. And if the average slips to 40/60 or 30/70 for any length of time, then I say to myself, *Florine, you're going to have to make some changes in this relationship.* Maybe it means sitting down with that person to figure out what is going on and trying to work things out.

You know what? I found out that it can't be right for me and wrong for him, just as it can't be right for him and wrong for me.

Respect has to be a mutual give-and-take. Remember, the 70/30 Rule applies to us, too. I ask and hope that the people around me overlook my 20 percent or 30 percent—the times when I push their buttons by saying or doing something I shouldn't have—and dwell on my 70 percent or 80 percent—the good times that we have together. It takes two people to talk it out, to work it out, and to compromise here and there . . . until you get to that place where it's right for both of you.

Disagreements

Working it out may lead to disagreements. You may even argue—and that's okay, too. But there is a universal rule about arguments. Everybody wants to be right. Once you recognize and accept this, you will realize that there is rarely a way to *win* an argument. No matter how it's left, you'll probably walk away believing you're right and he will walk away believing he's right. And that's okay—as long as no one is being hurt. That's just agreeing to disagree.

Whenever possible, my husband and I avoided arguing by agreeing that he'd do it his way and I'd do it my way. There were plenty of other times that we were able to agree and did things our way.

After a hard day's work, I love to get into bed, prop up my pillows, and enjoy a nighttime snack while I read a book or watch TV. That's been my special comfort and stress-reliever for as long as I can remember. Of course, the snack used to be a half gallon of ice cream, but now I count my points (from the Weight Watchers program) and know what I can or can't have, and whatever I choose to eat, I enjoy every minute of it. My husband only ate in the kitchen. He'd occasionally look at me and say, "Don't you think that eating is for in the kitchen?" I'd remind him that for me eating is for in the kitchen *and* in bed at the end of the day as a stress-reliever. He may not have been crazy about the idea of eating in bed, but he knew that I was. We both had our views on where food did and didn't belong, and we both knew that neither of us was going to change how the other one felt about it. We agreed to disagree. I ate my snack in bed—that was part of the 20 percent or 30 percent of my day with him that he didn't like—and he chose to overlook it.

If we did have an argument—I like to think of it as a passionate discussion rather than an argument—we'd go to the mirror together. You can try this, too. Go over to the mirror with your loved one, hold hands, and watch your own reflections while you talk about the issue. Most times, you won't be able to do this without laughing. It breaks the intensity of your focus and gives you both the chance to realize that what you're arguing about probably isn't that important. In the grand scheme of things, it might even seem downright silly. When it isn't a silly argument, you may be able to resolve the disagreement by looking into each other's eyes and talking it out. And if that doesn't work, try to put the subject away for another day and refocus on that 70 percent or 80 percent or 90 percent of what you love about each other instead of what you don't like about each other at that specific moment.

Moving on from a Relationship

For all of these strategies, you may still find yourself in dark times when you truly aren't being loved or appreciated, and nothing you try changes it. You can't *make* someone love you or behave in a loving way. I hope you never find yourself in that situation, but if you do, remember: *you have no power over what people say or do, but you do have power over how you react to what people say or do.* You deserve to be loved and nurtured. If you're giving love but are unable to get love in return, you may need to give less to that person, spend less time with that person, or, if being with that person has become harmful to your well-being and you've tried *everything* but can't work it out, you may have to walk away from the relationship.

All relationships are important, but we have to know when we've done our best and it's time to move on. This was a lesson that Lisa Avery, one of the Remarkable Women I've been privileged to interview on my syndicated radio show, *Remarkable Woman*, learned during a painful marriage. Lisa had little experience with the world when she met and married her husband. It was too late when she realized that he was an alcoholic. Lisa—who was a stay-at-home mom—had no job and felt she didn't have any qualifications to get one. She had no family to turn to. All this combined to make Lisa feel trapped in her marriage. She tried to work things out by being a loving wife and encouraging him to seek help. Unfortunately, he didn't want help, and as he began to drink more and more, Lisa's husband became violent, nearly killing her four times during the course of their marriage. Although her husband had never hit the children, Lisa realized it was only a matter of time before he did. That realization gave her the courage to get her children and herself out of this terrible situation.

Lisa left her husband, and for a month, she asked several people she knew to let her children and her stay with them while she looked for work. When fear and doubt would start to creep in, Lisa would say to herself over and over, *If you want it bad enough, you can do anything.* Sure enough, she found a job and in time built a new life for her children and herself. Today Lisa owns a successful business and is married to a man she loves—and who loves her back. She has achieved balance in her life—giving others kind and loving treatment and expecting her own kind and loving treatment in return.

Treat Yourself Well

Interestingly, Lisa's journey to achieving that balance began with the third side of the Golden Triangle: treat yourself as well as you treat everyone else. Lisa said of her first marriage, "I felt lost and devastated when I realized that my first husband didn't love me. Worse, I had stopped loving myself. I hated myself for letting this happen." She had to learn to believe in herself again before she could change her life (and the lives of her children). She had to befriend herself—recognizing and appreciating her own strengths and forgiving herself for making mistakes—before she could develop the confidence to find a job and start a new life.

Many times we are much harder on ourselves than we are on others. If someone bumps into me on the street and says to me, "Oh, I'm sorry," I say, "That's all right. Don't worry about it." I forgive him instantly and don't give it another thought. But if I make a mistake—eating something I shouldn't have, putting off a project that I know I need to start, making a bad decision at work, saying something I wish I hadn't—it takes so much more effort for me to forgive myself.

I used to stew over those mistakes for hours—even days—which only made me feel worse. It wasted a perfectly beautiful day.

Now I allow myself *not* to be perfect. I take out the list that we made in chapter 2 and look it over. After I acknowledge that 20 percent or 30 percent of the things about me that I'd like to change, I also take a long look at the 70 percent or 80 percent that make me a good person. I remind myself that my mistake is over and done with. There is nothing I can do about it . . . *except* for one thing. I have the power to refuse to let anything negative that happened yesterday dampen my spirits today— and you have the same power.

I learned another *Talk to the Mirror* trick from Kitty Carlisle, a great actress and humanitarian. Kitty is a person who talks to the mirror every day. First thing in the morning, she looks squarely in the mirror and says, "Kitty, yesterday is over. Whatever mistakes you made yesterday, anything you may have said or done that was wrong, I forgive you. Today is a new day and a new beginning." To say that, to own it, to make it part of your being is so freeing and so true. Give yourself the same freedom to make mistakes that you give everyone else. And remember, nobody is perfect.

We also need to be our own caregivers. We make sure that our children (or even our pets) get enough exercise, our husbands or friends eat a healthy diet, and our parents get enough rest. But so few of us think we deserve the same. It reminds me of a truly gifted hairdresser I knew. Women left her shop looking like movie stars, but she never used her remarkable talents to do her own hair. Sure, it was clean and combed, but it had no style to it whatsoever. "I guess I don't think my hair is worth the time," she once said. My view is, as the hair-color commercial says, she's worth it. She's worth it, you're worth it, and I'm worth it.

Love yourself enough to keep your body healthy with exercise and a good, nutritionally balanced diet. Take those few extra minutes to prepare a healthy meal. The average person walks only 2,000 steps each day. Good health requires that we take at least *10,000* steps a day. Walk to your job or park your car a block away from your destination—these little extra efforts work together to make our bodies the best they can be. We deserve to live and feel our best.

And we deserve to relax. Take the daily hour we talked about in chapter 2. Tuck *yourself* into bed for seven or eight hours of sleep at night. Be the caregiver to yourself that you are to everyone else.

The Gift of Time

And finally, we need to give ourselves the gift of time. We're certainly willing to give time to everyone else. Whether it's a spouse, a lover, a friend, a child, a coworker, an employer, a needy member of the community—their lack of planning is our emergency. We dish out large slices of time, all the time—often without even thinking about it. Of course, there is time that we *have* to give to others. We have to earn a living, we have to help a small child get dressed. But if we take stock of the time we give to others every day, most of us will find that we're giving more than we have to . . . and maybe we're giving more time than we can afford.

We tend to treat time as if we have a limitless supply. Even though we know in our minds that no one lives forever, few, if any, of us are truly prepared for the day when time—when life—runs out. Jeannette was my good friend for many years. She was always vibrant and healthy. One day she complained that she wasn't feeling well. By the next day she was in the hospital, and a few weeks later she died of cancer. Jeannette never even knew she had the disease—it was a form of cancer that had very few symptoms until the end. After her funeral, I wondered how Jeannette would have spent the last weeks or month or year of her life if she'd known how little time she'd had left. How many things had she been putting off that suddenly would have become her highest priorities? Whom would she have called? How many people would she have told she loved them? Were there broken relationships she'd have tried to mend? How many things had she been doing every day that suddenly would have become totally unimportant? What was on her calendar for the month that she would have canceled?

But Jeannette didn't know that she had so little time left. And the difficult truth is that none of us knows, either. So ask yourself, if you knew you had only one week (or month, or year) left, what would be important? What would be worth your time then? When you've answered those questions, you'll know how you should be spending more of your time right now. Don't worry if your priorities don't seem important to someone else. Maybe you've always wanted to learn to knit or you like walking in the rain. Maybe gardening gives you great joy, or you've always wondered what it would be like to scuba dive. Maybe you've always wanted to see a kangaroo up close. These are *your* priorities and the things that you should find the time to do in your life.

And if it turns out that you've got another fifty or more years of living (and I wish that for all of us!) and you spend your time doing more of the things that matter to you most, with the people who matter to you most, think of how wonderful those years will be!

EXERCISE: How Does Your Golden Triangle Shape Up?

1. Begin by drawing your own triangle. Make sure that there is plenty of room to write underneath your triangle and to the left and right of it.

2. Underneath the foundation, list all the things that you do to make life better for others. Don't worry about listing them in any order or whether they're big or small. Maybe you donate cookies to church events, do laundry for your family, iron your husband's shirts, drive your child (and maybe the neighbor's children) to soccer practice, agree to switch days off with a coworker, help your girlfriend move to a new apartment. List whatever comes to mind for five minutes.

3. On the left side of the triangle, list all the nice things you can think of that others do for you. Again, they don't have to be big. Maybe a coworker brought you a cup of coffee

when you were swamped. Your husband might have put the kids to bed so you could have a girls' night out. Your mother might have had you over to dinner. Really brainstorm this for five minutes.

4. Finally, on the right side of the triangle, write down all the things that you do for yourself. You might include getting a facial, manicure, or massage; taking time to read a good book; walking several times a week; making yourself a special salad (baby spinach with mushrooms, dried cranberries, a sprinkling of chopped pecans, and balsamic vinaigrette is a nice change!); indulging in a bubble bath; enjoying a hobby. Again, give this activity five minutes.

5. Now take a look at your triangle. If your list at the bottom is significantly longer than either or both of your other lists, it's time to think about some changes. Giving to others is so important, but also receiving from others and giving to yourself will bring the balance to your life you need to be happy, healthy, and whole.

Some Great Resources

Difficult Conversations: How to Discuss What Matters Most by Douglas Stone

Honoring the Self by Nathaniel Branden

Love Yourself, Heal Your Life Workbook by Louise L. Hay and Glenn Kolb

Say Please, Say Thank You: The Respect We Owe One Another by Donald W. McCullough

Stick Up for Yourself: Every Kid's Guide to Personal Power and Positive Self-Esteem by Gershen Kaufman (written for kids but a great read for grown-ups, too!)

A Worthy Woman by Gail Majcher

5

Just Being Me

Until you make peace with who you are,
you'll never be content with what you have.
—Doris Mortman from Circles

If you do not ask yourself what it is you know,
you will go on listening to others and change will not
come because you will not hear your own truth.
—St. Bartholomew

It isn't where you came from.
It's where you're going that counts.
—Ella Fitzgerald

The miracle is this—the more we share, the more we have.
—Leonard Nimoy

MORE THAN EIGHTY YEARS AGO, Susan B. Anthony and her suffragettes won the right for women to vote. And

I can't imagine that any of us would give up that right today. So why do we still give up the right to vote on how we run our own lives? We spend too much time listening to what everyone else thinks we should do, instead of listening to what we *want* to do. As a result, we sometimes ruin good relationships with ourselves and others because we get mixed up about who we are and what we really want.

I've already admitted that I don't feel fulfilled being a full-time homemaker. Now I know that's okay. But I had to come to terms with wanting a career, because in my generation, a woman was made to feel guilty if she wasn't a stay-at-home mom. Some women are happiest being full-time homemakers, and that's perfectly right for them. At least it should be. But too often I hear women saying, "'They' say that today women *have* to work outside the home to make ends meet," or "'They' say that children need to have a stay-at-home mom." "They" always have something to say . . . but who are "they," anyway? And what makes "them" so knowledgeable about what's best for you or me? You've got to figure out for yourself what makes you happy and fulfilled, then make a plan and go do it. If it doesn't work out, that's okay, too. The only failure is in *not* trying. Just make a new plan and keep trying until you find what works for you.

Gaining Experience

First things first, though: how do you figure out what really makes you happy? I believe that to make smart decisions about who we are and what we want, we have to know something about what's out there. We have to drink in life's experiences, and there are a number of ways to do that.

One way to gain experience is through education. I try to learn as much as I can. It expands my horizons and provides me with a wealth of experience and stimulation. Learning shouldn't end just because school does. I surround myself with people who know things I don't know, and I learn from them. At the office, I learn from experts in marketing, law, finance, and business development. At home, I learn from experts in cooking when I read new recipes or watch cooking shows on television. I learn about plumbing and electrical wiring when service people come to make repairs. I want to be learning as long as I'm living.

Another way to drink in life experiences—and lifelong learning—is by reading. I read biographies, mysteries, histories, self-help books—I'm a voracious reader. Books help me to live a fuller life by learning new things and by reading about people's lives and adventures that otherwise I may never experience in my lifetime. I never met Winston Churchill, but I've always been fascinated by the man. I've read so many books about his life that I feel in some ways as if I know him. Learning more about his life experiences—as well as many others—gives me insight into my own life.

Their stories comfort and inspire me when I'm living through difficult times in my own life. When I read that Winston Churchill—and so many others throughout history—weathered tough times to live happier days, it gives me a little more courage and makes me feel that I'm not alone. It makes me feel that if they can do it, then I can do it, too.

Travel can provide even more life experiences. When my husband and I visited other places, he always wanted to see museums and churches. They were beautiful, but to be honest, I could only visit so many of them before I wanted to go to the shops, supermarkets, and department stores. My husband would roll his eyes and say, "You just want to go shopping." Well, yes I did—and do—like to shop . . . but it's a bit more than that. I love to see other people's art, the foods they eat, how they dress—I want to listen to what they have to say and even the way they speak. To me, *living* is an art museum. Instead of looking at art painted on canvas, I'm fascinated by the fabric that people have woven into their lives. It's always exciting to me when people invite me into their homes when I'm traveling. That's when I really get to see how they live . . . from the colors and styles they use to decorate their homes to the family traditions they honor. I want to see what we do the same and what we do differently. To me, that's art. Drinking in their day-to-day life tells me something about them, and ultimately it tells me something about me. It opens my eyes up to new experiences that I can bring home to make my everyday life better and more fulfilling.

And if you really want more life experience, volunteer for a charitable cause that is completely new to you. I've been on both sides of charity—I've given and when our family needed help, we got it. When I was growing up and my sister was in the hospital for two years with polio, we needed help to give her the medical care she needed. I'm thankful every day for the charitable organizations that helped our family during that difficult time. When I started working, I started volunteering—to give back some of what our family was given. Giving money to charities is an important gift to those in need; but giving your time is as valuable a gift for them *and* for you. Get to know the people you're volunteering to help—what's important to them, what kind of obstacles they face, what kind of resources they have. You'll help them and learn some things about yourself. As Churchill said, "We make a living by what we get; we make a life by what we give."

Try Something New, but . . .

Along the way, you'll learn what you like in your life—and what you don't like in your life. For instance, I don't like to ski.

I'm an athletic person—I play tennis, I golf, I run, I walk, I love to dance—but I don't like to ski. And it's not just the skiing itself. I don't like going up on ski lifts—I don't like being stuck in those little chairs as they sway back and forth, and I don't like the push you get when you're trying to get out of them at the top. I don't even like to watch skiing on television. But for years, I tried to ski. I'd join a ski clinic for a day, work with an instructor—but not once did I enjoy the experience of being on those slopes. I'd make myself miserable for two weeks before the ski trip thinking about it, and I'd be miserable for the whole trip. The only pleasurable time I had was when I got back home and the experience was over. So why did I do it? Well, my husband skied. Our friends skied. We planned entire vacations around skiing. They loved it, so I felt guilty that I didn't love it. That's why I gave it my all for so many years.

Finally, about four years ago I said to myself, *That's it. Florine, you've tried long enough and hard enough to know that you are never going to like skiing.* I explained to my husband that I had given skiing a fair try—more than a fair try— and I just didn't like it. In fact, I hated it. While I appreciated that he loved it, my skiing days were over. He was surprised, but he understood. We still took skiing vacations with our friends. But while they were skiing, I was walking or shopping or enjoying a manicure at the spa. I didn't spoil their fun, but I made sure that I had a good time, too. That way we were all happy. We got together on our trips to do the things we all enjoy—like talking and laughing and eating!

Don't be afraid to try something new. But if you don't like it, feel free to stop what you're doing at any time. It took me awhile to learn that concept . . . and I don't just mean with skiing. It used to be that if I started a book, I felt as if I had to finish it, even if I didn't like it. Otherwise, I felt like I was cheating or wasting my money. Then I learned to speed-read, and if I wasn't crazy about a book, I'd catch myself speed-reading through it. One day I was speed-reading and thought, I really don't like this book at all, so I read the last three pages to see how it ended and then I put the book down. I realized that all that time I'd kept reading because stopping felt like admitting I'd made a mistake and wouldn't that be terrible? I thought of it as failure if I put the book down when I didn't like it, when it was really having the good sense to know when something wasn't right for me, letting it go, and moving on. Life is like reading a book—if you don't like what you're reading, skip to the next chapter. If that doesn't work, don't "go by the book"—start a *new* book. Start a new phase of your life or a new project. Don't get down on yourself if you decide not to finish something you start and don't like. It should be just the opposite. Pat yourself on the back and say, Wasn't I smart? I didn't waste days, months, or even years doing something that I didn't like. What's important is that you gave what you wanted to do a try and you recognized that it wasn't right for you. And by the way, that includes this book. If you're not getting anything out of it, put it down or give it to someone else. I won't take it personally—life is too short.

Very often, we already know the answer to who we are and what we want to do. Somehow we just know it in our hearts and in our guts. General Norman Schwarzkopf once said, "The truth of the matter is that you almost always know the right thing to do. The hard part is doing it."

Don't Be Afraid!

A lot of us are afraid of life. We're afraid to try something new even when, in our hearts, we have the feeling that it's right for us. But if we don't try the things we want to do because we're afraid, we'll never grow into who we want to be. That includes doing things that "they" might think we can't do. History is full of visionaries who changed the world by seeing possibilities when everyone else thought it could never be done. When Thomas Edison was asked how he successfully invented the lightbulb when so many had failed, he said it was because he hadn't read all the research that said it couldn't be done so he just did it. Be innovative. If you have an idea for a new product or service or a new way to work at home, don't assume it won't work because it's never been done before. Where would we be if everyone let that fear hold them back? We'd not only be in the dark because there would be no lightbulbs, we'd be in the Dark Ages. There would be no cars, no television, no computers, no X-rays . . . no modern medicine or technology of any kind. Someone had to say "I've got an idea," and then have the courage to bring that idea to life—while "they" were telling them it could never be done.

Choose Who *You* Want to Be

A lot of us are also afraid to think outside the box—even when we know in our hearts that to do so is right for us. Just a few generations ago, women didn't have a choice about whether they should stay at home or get a job. Staying at home was our job. Men didn't have a choice either—they were expected to have jobs. "They" set rules for the roles that men and women were supposed to live by—even when some men were better nurturers and some women had a better head for business. Whole families suffered because "they" dictated that people stay in their mismatched roles. While it's become commonplace to see women working outside the home, we're just now starting to see stay-at-home dads. It still takes courage and vision to reverse those roles, but for the first time in history, both men and women can choose who they want to be. We no longer have to let "them" decide what's right for us.

One of the first examples of reversing gender roles that I ever heard was a story about John Lennon and Yoko Ono. I read that when their son was born, Yoko turned to John and said, "I carried him for nine months. Now it's your turn." John became a stay-at-home dad, changing diapers, filling bottles, delighting in being there for all his son's "firsts." Yoko went to work and, by all accounts, grew their small fortune into a large one. I'm sure people talked. I'm also pretty sure that John and Yoko weren't interested in what "they" had to say. John and Yoko did what was right for them and their family—and they were all the happier for it.

A more recent example of role reversal—and an example of just *how much* roles are changing—happened right here in Michigan. In 2002, Jennifer Granholm became the first female governor of Michigan and her husband, Daniel Granholm Mulhern, became the First Gentleman. Rather than shying away from this role, Dan has embraced it with enthusiasm. He resigned from the consulting firm that he founded in 1999 to work full time as a "first spouse." He is a tireless volunteer for the state of Michigan, has taken over many of the parenting responsibilities for Jennifer's and his three children, and has hosted a series of forums that invited other men to talk about their own role-reversal situations. It takes courage, commitment, and more than a little humor to chart such new territory for gender roles, but Jennifer and Dan are doing it on their own terms.

That's not to say it's always easy. There will always be people who want to tell us how to live our lives. I know a woman named Erica who is a very successful teacher. Her husband, who is older than she is, is retired from the military. He can stay at home with the kids while she is now pursuing a career that she loves. They are very happy with their lifestyle, but Erica overheard a couple of women criticizing her family's living arrangement at a party. They didn't know that Erica was standing nearby when one asked the other, "What's wrong with him? Is he lazy?" "Doesn't he want to go out and support his family?" Erica was hurt, angry, and even a little embarrassed. But to her credit, Erica walked up to the women and calmly explained that this arrangement was right for her family. That takes a lot of courage. But we need to be like Erica—we need to decide what's right for us and stand up for our choices.

What's best for us isn't always going to be popular. Some people can be very critical. "They" want us to think inside the box. But don't let them dictate what you do—"they" don't live with the consequences or the rewards. You do.

While setting your course, it's important to remember that although men and women are equal—neither gender is better than the other—"equal" doesn't mean that men and women are the same. In some ways, we're very different. We all have our own strengths and weaknesses, our own likes and dislikes, our own gifts that we can use to make our lives and our family's lives better.

I learned this when one day I got tired of always being the one to make my husband's and my travel arrangements. I was the one who called the airline, got our tickets—I took care of it all. I was feeling overwhelmed with work and decided that this time, my husband should take charge of planning our trip. He handled the travel arrangements the way he thought best, which, to be honest, wasn't the way I would have handled them. My husband was more interested in looking at the big picture—he didn't like thinking about all the little details that planning a trip takes. He was more free-spirited. After that trip, we both realized that when I made the arrangements, we got to see and do more because I'm detail-oriented by nature. From that moment on, instead of keeping score, we each did whatever we did best and we both had a lot more fun. I made the travel arrangements, and he made each trip a special adventure for both of us.

Believe me, there were many things that my husband was better at than I was. Take grocery shopping, for instance. If we needed four oranges and my husband went to the supermarket to get them, he came back with four oranges. It might have cost us a couple of bucks. If I went to the store to get the four oranges, I'd see a new salad mix that looked good or a sweetener that I thought we should try—by the time I was done I'd spent fifty dollars. When it came to staying on a household budget or saving money at the supermarket, my husband won hands down.

Listen to Your Inner Voice

We were both okay admitting our strengths and weaknesses because we were comfortable with ourselves as individuals and as a couple. My husband was a doctor; he was also a self-trained pianist, artist, and photographer. I spend a lot of time doing public speaking, and I appear on television and on radio. He wasn't insecure about the time I spent in the limelight because he created his own limelight—he was accomplished in his own right. You can do the same. Find a niche. Become an authority on something that matters to you. Whether it's being the best kids' soccer coach in your neighborhood or the most organized manager in your office, do something that belongs to you and don't let anyone else tell you otherwise. You may be surprised at what you can accomplish when you listen to your inner voice.

Peggy's Story

Peggy Griffen is a Remarkable Woman and also a friend. She has many strengths, but the thing I admire most about her is that she always listens to her inner voice. I've never known Peggy to do anything based on what "they" thought she could or couldn't do. If she had, her life would probably have been very different.

I met Peggy at Harvard University when I attended a networking breakfast to mentor women who are graduate students at the Kennedy School of Government. Peggy is pursuing her master's degree in public administration and is expected to graduate in June 2004. She also works full time as a regional civil rights officer for the Federal Transit Administration of the U.S. Department of Transportation. Peggy is married to a wonderful man who became paralyzed from the waist down when he was shot while saving another soldier during the Vietnam War. Her husband earned a law degree *after* his paralysis, but until recently, he had been unable to work due to complications after triple bypass surgery. They have three children—triplets—two daughters and one son. *And Peggy has been legally blind since birth*. But for all those remarkable details, the most important part of her story is that Peggy loves her life.

Peggy learned at a young age to analyze her strengths and weaknesses, to make the most of her abilities, and to use them to live the life she wants. Her childhood eye doctor once told her, "Don't let your weaknesses be the defining thing about you. Make them just another part of your life." Peggy took that advice to heart and lives every day being (and still becoming!) the person she wants to be.

When I asked Peggy if she ever has doubts about what she can accomplish, she told me, "Almost never. And that's because I don't think in terms of 'I can't,' or 'Why did these things happen to me?' I think in terms of 'Why not me?', 'Why can't I try this?', and 'Why can't I accomplish this?' If I fail, so what? That just means I'm supposed to try something else." Rather than seeing her possibilities as being very limited, she sees her life as being full of all kinds of possibilities that she *can* accomplish. Peggy succeeds because she lives her life in terms of who she wants to be—fear of failure never enters her thinking.

There is another key to Peggy's long list of accomplishments.

Peggy always has a plan designed to move her closer to her goals. Making and following a daily plan can make the difference between living an ordinary life and an *extra*ordinary life. Having a plan keeps us focused on our goals and makes the most of our efforts to reach those goals every day.

So how do you start a plan? For starters, ask yourself two important questions. The first one is, what do I really want in life? And two, what am I willing to do to get it? A plan can become an accomplishment only when you know the answers to those two questions.

Be sure to set a time limit, since having a deadline will keep you from putting things off. You might even want to set time limits after each step of your plan so you can check to see how you're progressing, decide if you need to change your plan, or even start a new plan. Have a plan for *every day*—even if that plan is just to relax and rejuvenate, it's still a plan.

No plan would be complete without factoring in your priorities. Peggy had been planning to pursue a master's degree for a long time, but when her children were small, the timing wasn't right. Her daughters were born with the same condition that caused her blindness. When Peggy was born, the technology didn't exist to treat her. But by the time her girls were born, surgery was an option. After surgery, Peggy's girls needed her even more. They had to be her priority then. By the time her girls were thirteen (and seeing beautifully!) and able to take care of themselves and help out around the house, Peggy decided that the time was right for her to make her master's degree a priority.

Set Your Own Priorities

Setting priorities is a very personal decision. Take Sophie and Mabel, for example, two elderly ladies who go for a walk together every day. They're walking past a storefront when Sophie looks in the window and sees a beautiful hat for sale. They go inside and Sophie buys the hat and likes it so much that she wears it right out of the store. They continue their walk and the wind really starts blowing. Sophie doesn't want to lose her new hat so she's holding it on with both hands. Mabel yells, "Sophie, forget about the hat! Your skirt is blowing up and people can see your private parts!" Sophie yells back, "Forget about my private parts! They're eighty-five years old and this hat is brand-new!" That story always brings a smile to my face—how about you?

No one can set your priorities but you. Be honest with yourself about the things that really matter to you. Write them down to get a better look at your options, talk them over with yourself in the mirror (actually say them out loud!), work them into a plan, and put that plan into action.

Remember, only you can choose who are, what you're going to do, and what matters in your life—and it's your choice to make so that each day is the best it can be for you and those around you.

EXERCISE: One for You and One for Me

You can start doing more of the tasks you enjoy—and maybe less of the tasks you dislike—right now. Make a list of all the chores in your household. Then give a copy to everyone you live with (spouse, children, roommates—whoever they may be) along with the following directions. (Make sure you keep a copy for yourself to complete, too.)

Read over all the chores on the list. If you see a task that you really like to do or are especially good at doing, put a number 1 next to it. If you are somewhat good at it or like doing the task well enough, put a 2 next to it. If you'd really rather not do that task, but could do it if you had to, put a 3 next to it, and if you hate even the thought of it, put a 4 next to that chore.

Get together and compare lists. Divide up the 1's and 2's— that's the easy part. But there are almost always going to be 3's and 4's that overlap—tasks that nobody wants to do, like taking out the trash or cleaning the bathroom. Those are tasks that you may have to take turns doing. You might say, "I'll take the trash out the first and third weeks of the month if you'll take it out during the second and fourth weeks." This lets household members make the most of their strengths and enjoy things they like to do without others always getting stuck doing things they don't do well or just plain don't like to do at all.

If you live alone, you can still use this exercise. Take a look at the things you have listed as 3's and ask yourself what you can do to make the task more enjoyable. Maybe you don't really like to do dishes. One option is to use paper plates and cups so that you have fewer dishes to wash. Another option is playing music that you enjoy or putting a mini television on your counter to watch while you work.

When it comes to the 4's, first ask yourself if there is any way you can get around doing them. If you really hate to mow your lawn, maybe you can rework your budget to pay the neighbor's teenager to mow it for you. Maybe you can trade tasks with a neighbor or friend. You might also be able to find different ways of doing the task that will at least move it up to a 3. For instance, if you hate the thought of cleaning your shower doors, you may find a product at the supermarket to make the task faster or easier. And ultimately, if it's a job you detest but it has to be done, dig in and promise yourself to do something you really enjoy as soon as you're done. At least you'll have something to look forward to that you can be thinking about while you're working.

SELF-TEST: It's My Life . . . Isn't It?

Choose the sentence that best answers each of the following.

1. I chose the work I do because:
    a. Several people told me I'd be good at it.
    b. The work interests me or I think it's good experience for my dream job.
    c. Several people in my family are in the same line of work.

2. My home is decorated to reflect:
    a. Whatever is fashionable now.
    b. My taste if I live alone, or a combination of my taste and my spouse's (roommate's or significant other's) taste.
    c. My spouse's taste.

3. A friend or family member is openly critical of a choice that I make (at work, in child-rearing, and so on). I listen to her point of view but find that I completely disagree. I'm most likely to:
    a. Feel hurt or angry and worry that she disapproves of me.
    b. Calmly tell her that I understand what she's saying, I disagree, and I have to do what I think is right for me.
    c. Change the choice I made to keep the peace.

4. I work in a job that although it's not very exciting, has a good salary with benefits and is fairly secure. I'm offered my dream job, but it's a newly created position in an environment that is completely unfamiliar to me. I:
    a. Pass. It's too much of a risk.
    b. Make a list of pros and cons, think about what matters most to me, and make a choice. Whatever happens, no regrets.
    c. Ask a colleague what she would do.

5. At a party, a small group of us are talking politics. Everyone else seems to be in favor of the issue, while I'm definitely opposed. I:
    a. Move to another group as inconspicuously as possible.
    b. Tell them that I have to disagree and politely offer my view.
    c. Change the subject as quickly as possible.

Analysis

Go for the b's on this test. They show that in these situations, you take responsibility for your own life and your own views. You're neither passive nor aggressive—you're doing what you believe is right for you.

Some Great Resources

Do What You Love, The Money Will Follow: Discovering Your Right Livelihood by Marsha Sinetar

I Don't Know What I Want, but I Know It's Not This: A Step-By-Step Guide to Finding Gratifying Work by Julie Jansen

Making Peace with Yourself by Harold H. Bloomfield

The Nine Modern Day Muses: 10 Guides to Creative Inspiration for Artists, Poets, Lovers, and Other Mortals Wanting to Live a Dazzling Existence by Jill Baldwin Badonsky

The Practical Dreamer's Handbook: Finding the Time, Money, and Energy to Live the Life You Want to Live by Paul Edwards and Sarah Edwards

PART II

WHEN LIFE THROWS YOU
A CURVEBALL

*I have always grown from my problems
and challenges, from the things that don't
work out. That's when I've really learned.*
—CAROL BURNETT

A diamond is a chunk of coal that made good under pressure.
—ANONYMOUS

*I live by one principle: enjoy life with no conditions!
That is the one thing I hope to have contributed to
my children, by example and by talk: to make no
conditions, to understand that life is a wonderful
thing and to enjoy it, every day, to the full.*
—ARTUR RUBENSTEIN

WHEN YOU'RE STANDING IN LINE at the supermarket or sitting in a waiting room for an appointment, do you find yourself drawn to the magazines that tell all about movie stars, artists, models, and musicians? You know the people I'm talking about—the thin, rich, and famous? If you do, you're not alone. So many of us are captivated by these people that entire television shows, newspapers, and magazines are devoted to keeping us informed about their every move. We know all about the projects they're working on, the fashions they wear, how they keep their figures, who they're dating or married to, and what they think about a wide variety of subjects. I probably know more about Brad Pitt and Jennifer Aniston—who live on the other side of the country—than I do about people who live a couple of blocks away from me. Why are we so curious about people we've never even met?

Mostly I'd say it's because we want to be like them. The media are constantly showing us a long list of benefits that go with being thin, rich, and famous. From the outside, it seems that if you're thin, rich, and famous, everyone knows and adores you, nearly everything you say is newsworthy, and you can have whatever you want. It's a lot like being popular in high school—except on a global scale. Like many little girls and young women, I grew up dreaming of being one of those thin, beautiful movie stars. I thought that if I could be thin, rich, and famous, my life would be just perfect.

Today I've made some headway in realizing those dreams. I'm fit and trim, I own a very successful business, and while I didn't become a movie star, people recognize me and talk to me as if they know me almost everywhere I go. I'm here to tell you it *is* a great life to have. But there is one thing that it's not—and that's perfect.

The truth is that if you had the face of an angel, the body of a lingerie model, the money of a Silicon Valley king, and a marriage made in heaven, life would still find a way to throw you a curveball. That's just the way it is.

Movie-star marriages fail, world-class athletes contract life-threatening illnesses, and millionaires file for bankruptcy. The only thing that's different about the curveballs that life throws the rich and famous is that very often their painful moments are lived in the public eye and often on a grander scale. Warren Buffett, who was named 2003's most powerful businessperson in America by *Fortune* magazine, summed it up when he said, "It really just means that if I do something dumb, I can do it on a very big scale. It means you could add a lot of zeros to the losses."

No matter who you are, there are going to be times when life is not fair. No one wears magic armor that protects her from life's curveballs. And when those curveballs come, we're not separated by how good we look in a swimsuit, how many people know who we are, or how much money we have. We're separated by how we choose to handle the curveballs that come flying our way.

Lou Gehrig is remembered less for being a great baseball player than he is for the bravery and dignity he showed when he had to quit the game because he had contracted amyotrophic lateral sclerosis (ALS), a degenerative neurological disease. Christopher Reeve isn't as highly regarded for playing Superman as he is for the determination he has shown in coping with the almost total paralysis he suffered in a horse-riding accident. Michael J. Fox, who is battling Parkinson's disease, may have starred in a number of hit films, but today people are talking more about the book he has written about his life and the fact that he chose to title it *Lucky Man*. Long after batting averages and box-office draws are forgotten, these people will be remembered for their *extraordinary* responses to life's curveballs.

How do you want to live your life? Are you willing to settle for sitting back helplessly watching as life just happens to you? Are you going to whine and pace the floor, telling yourself and everyone else how unfair life is? Or do you want to live an extraordinary life, catching as many of those curveballs as you can and learning how to cope with the ones that get past you?

The chapters in this part are all about managing life's challenging times by taking control of what you can, learning ways to cope with the things you can't control, and sometimes even using life's unexpected downturns to make your life fuller and richer in the long run. All you need is this book, a pen and paper for some self-tests and personal exercises, and of course your mirror.

Let's play ball!

6

C-H-A-N-G-E—for Some People, It's a Four-Letter Word

Without change, there would be no butterflies.
—Unknown

Our dilemma is that we hate change and love it at the same time; what we want is for things to remain the same but get better.
—Sydney Harris

It's not that some people have willpower and some don't. It's that some people are ready to change and others are not.
—Dr. James Gordon

How wonderful it is that nobody need wait a single moment before beginning to improve the world.
—Anne Frank

I T IS OFTEN SAID THAT the two things that people are most afraid of are public speaking and death—in that order. But you never hear much about what's number three on the list of people's greatest fears. Well, I think it's *change*. I don't just mean tragic change or unforeseen change. I mean any change. Whether it's change that's good for us, change that's bad for us, change we want, change we don't want, change we've been expecting, or change we never saw coming—people spend an enormous amount of energy every day fearing and even fighting change.

And I don't know why. Some people say they dread change because it means stepping into the unknown. But every day that we get out of bed, we're stepping into the unknown. That's life! Change is what gives us the chance to grow and to improve ourselves in any situation. Without change, I'd still be the overweight, insecure, lonely Florine I was when I was growing up. I wouldn't have my five children (or my nineteen grandchildren), I wouldn't have married my husband, Bill, and I wouldn't have founded my company, which has brought me great personal joy and enabled me to help so many others to live happier and healthier lives. I love change. But for all that, I have to admit that sometimes change scares me, too. If you don't love change—if even the thought of change either frightens or exhausts you—the first thing you need to change is your attitude about it.

You can talk yourself into feeling good about making a change by taking control of what you can to make changes in your life work for you. Let's say, for example, that you've just been promoted at work. It's the dream job you've always wanted, the pay is great, and you have a terrific staff. But you're a night person—you've always worked a 10 A.M. to 6 P.M. schedule. Your new boss wants you to be at work by eight in the morning. You can worry endlessly about not being able to become a morning person—or you can embrace the change. You have to ask yourself, how much do you want all the good things that come with this job? Are all those good things worth it to you to make the change? For me, the answer would be yes.

Focus on the Benefits

Start by focusing on what you're getting out of the change—in this case, it's the promotion, the money, and the people you'll be working with—and *decide* that maybe giving up your night life is really worth it to be able to enjoy all the benefits that come with the new job and early mornings. Then take control of what you can. Program your VCR to tape your late-night shows and watch them over the weekend. During the week, set your alarm earlier. As soon as you get up, go to the mirror and tell yourself how lucky you are to have this day. Say to yourself, "I am so lucky to see another sunrise and to have this terrific job to go to. I may have to be at work two hours earlier, but I'll be done two hours earlier, too. This is going to be a great day!" Then do some exercise to really get your blood moving. Shower, dress, and eat a healthy breakfast. By the time you head out the door to go to work, you'll be wide awake and in a much more positive frame of mind than if you'd slept in until the last minute, frantically rushed to get ready, skipping breakfast and worrying the whole way to the office that you'd be late. You can't control the change in your work hours, but you can control the way you respond to the change. You can *decide* to change from being a night person to being a morning person.

Making a lasting change—whether it's becoming a morning person, quitting smoking, taking an hour for yourself every day, changing your eating habits, exercising more, or just about anything else—takes time and effort. I read somewhere that it takes at least four months—sixteen weeks—of repeating a new behavior day in and day out, until you do it automatically. It becomes a part of you—you own it. In the meantime, go to that mirror every day and remind yourself that you can do it. You *can* do anything you want if you want to do it bad enough. It's really your choice.

Now you may be saying to yourself, *Florine doesn't know what she's talking about. I can't do that.* Oh yes you can! You can, if you know what four times five equals. Of course, you know it equals twenty—but *how* did you know that? You knew because at some point in your life, a teacher made you write down or repeat your multiplication tables over and over. He or she made you practice, practice, practice until the answers became an automatic response. That method works for any change in our behavior that we want to make—however big or small the change may be. It's practice, practice, practice until that change becomes a habit. Mark Twain got it right when he said, "Habit is habit and not to be flung out of the window by any man, but coaxed downstairs a step at a time."

As you know, I'm a big fan of walking. I walk between fifteen and twenty miles every week, mostly around my neighborhood or on my treadmill. While I walk, I keep my elbows bent and pump my arms because it uses more oxygen and burns more calories. I've used that walking technique for years—most of the time, I'm not even aware I'm pumping my arms. A few weeks ago, while I was on my walk, a neighbor stopped me to say good morning. He surprised me a little when he added, "Florine, did you know that you're holding your arms wrong when you walk?" Well, I'm always interested in making my workouts more effective so I asked him what I was doing wrong. He said, "When you bend your elbows like that, you build tension in your shoulders. You should let your arms hang down and swing them back and forth like a pendulum. You'll still burn extra calories but you won't tense up."

I thanked him very much and thought about what he'd said as I continued on my walk. His theory made a lot of sense, so I decided to give the new technique a try. It seemed like such a simple change to make, so I started walking, swinging my arms like a pendulum. So far, so good. Then my mind started to wander; I was daydreaming as I often do during my walk. All at once, I realized I was bending and pumping my arms again. I had no idea how long I'd been bending and pumping them, but there I was, pumping away. I forced myself to go back to swinging my arms. Five minutes later, I looked down and there I was, pumping away again. I thought, *Florine, this is going to be a tough habit to break*. And it has been tough. I still have to remind myself to keep my arms more at my side. It takes constant reinforcement. It's that way anytime you want to change something that you've been doing for a long time—even something as small as swinging your arms.

So you might ask, is it really worth all that bother? Absolutely! In time, the small changes we make add up to better lifestyles and happier lives. I didn't lose fifty pounds and become physically fit by making one or two big changes. I made lots of little changes that when combined added up to a whole new lifestyle.

Changes in Eating Habits

One of the changes I made was giving up my four o'clock candy bars. Late afternoon has always been a rough time of day for me. From the time I was twenty years old to this very day, I find myself running out of steam at 4 P.M. For years, I would tell myself that the way to get that energy back was to eat a candy bar. I'd perk right up as soon as I ate that candy—but only for a half hour at the most. As soon as that sugar rush was over, I was just as tired as before—even more tired. So I'd have another candy bar. Not only was I tired again a half hour later, I felt terrible about myself. You can imagine what two candy bars a day did to my weight. I knew I had to make a change, and I decided to make it. I went to Weight Watchers. I went to the meetings, listened to the leaders, and learned so many wonderful ways that I could make positive changes—if I *wanted* to make them—to have a better life every day. And that's what's important—making changes so that life will be better every day.

Now, instead of stocking up on candy, I cut up fresh vegetables, put them in a bag, and take them to work with me every day. When 4 P.M. rolls around, I snack on those veggies with a glass of water or a cup of tea.

When I first started doing this, I still wanted the candy. A red pepper—no matter how delicious—does not taste the same as a chocolate bar. But I'd go to the mirror and tell myself that the vegetables I'm eating at four will make me look better and feel better . . . and I sure will feel better about myself when I wake up the next day.

When I'd wake up the next morning after all that candy, I'd say to myself, *Florine, why did you do this? You wanted to lose weight and you failed again. You just can't get this right. You blew it again. You are so stupid.* Those were terrible things to say to myself (and they're terrible things to say to yourself). Not only is talking like that forgetting to be our own best friends, but what we tell ourselves is how we act. How we act is who we become.

It's a much happier talk with the mirror when I spend it telling myself how vegetables make me stronger, they're good for my vision, they're good for my skin, they're full of antioxidants, and so on.

Eventually, I found out two things about myself. First, what

I was really craving at 4 P.M. every day was the comfort that I find in eating. Putting food in my mouth—whether it was candy or veggies—gave me that satisfaction. The second thing I found out was that when I chose the veggies instead of the candy, I liked myself so much more. That four o'clock veggie break became a lasting change. To this day, if you walk into my office at four, you'll find me eating my bag of vegetables.

As I said, my 4 P.M. vegetable break is just one of the many changes I made. I also changed the way I think about eating fatty foods. I talk to myself about how lots of fat in my diet isn't good for me. I talk to myself about the thick, yellow gunk that fat in my foods builds up in my veins—how it will block my arteries and keep my heart from getting the blood I needed to live. It is aversion therapy at its best. Once I am really able to envision those fats invading my veins and hurting my body, it reminds me why I made changes to my eating habits. I miss eating loads of ice cream and chicken with the skin on it, but I don't have those foods because I'd rather have a good chance to live a long, healthy life instead. I want to eat food that does me good.

I had to give up some foods altogether—like ice cream— because I learned the hard way that I can't have just one serving of them and be satisfied. I decided to drink more water—it helps me to feel more full. I started exercising every day. I had to give up certain foods because even at my goal weight, I have high cholesterol.

I can honestly tell you that it's been worth all the time and the effort to make those changes. I'm a happier person now. I smile more. I laugh more. I have more fun. It's hard to have fun when you're always telling yourself that you're a failure. It's a lot easier to be happy when you can say, I did it! I broke that candy habit and ate the vegetables that were good for me. I'm not a loser—I'm a *winner*!

I also have to tell you that if I'd tried to make all those changes at once, I would have failed. It would have been just too overwhelming for me. I didn't learn all my multiplication tables all at once, either. I mastered all the two's first, then went on to the three's, and so on. I mastered each of my weight-loss and fitness changes in the very same way . . . little by little, one day at a time.

You Can Change, Too!

You can make changes the same way. Start with a small change that you can commit to doing every day. Before you know it, sixteen weeks will be over, you'll really own that change, and you'll have the confidence to go on to more, maybe even bigger, changes.

My Coffee Story

We have to have a reason to make a change. That reason is our fuel, motivating us to keep our commitment to change. Let me give you an example of exactly what I mean. I used to be a serious coffee drinker, but twenty years ago, I decided to give it up. To this day, a lot of people think I gave coffee up as part of my commitment to a healthy lifestyle, but actually, health had nothing to do with it.

Even though I've been through two divorces, I've never believed in divorcing my husbands' families. I really enjoyed spending time with my ex-husband's mother and visited her often at the senior complex where she lived. In those days, Dunkin' Donuts coffee was a staple for me. I even took coffee with me when I visited my mother-in-law. I didn't think I drank that much—maybe four or five cups a day—but my husband said it was more like ten or twelve cups a day. My mother-in-law was always asking me to give up coffee—she said it just wasn't good for me. I always said, "No, Ma, I can't give up my coffee. It just gives me the boost I need during the day and besides, black coffee has no calories."

Not long after one of those visits to my mother-in law, my husband, Bill, and I went on our first trip to Europe, a trip I'd been dreaming of for years. We were in Paris when suddenly I got sick. I have to tell you that I rarely get sick; it's even more rare that I throw up, but at 2 A.M., I got out of bed and that's exactly what I did. The next morning I still wasn't feeling well so I stayed in the hotel room. We had promised our kids when we left that we wouldn't call them to check in while we were away. But I broke that promise—I just felt an almost over-whelming need to call home.

When I did call, I told them about how I had gotten so sick the night before. My son said, "Well, Mom, at about the same time that you were getting sick, Grandma was passing away in her sleep." I felt awful—I had loved my mother-in-law dearly. I wanted to come right home, but my kids asked me not to. They said that she wouldn't want that, that she was well into her nineties and had had a good life. She'd known how I'd dreamt of this trip. Reluctantly, I agreed to stay where I was.

I asked my husband to take me to a synagogue in Paris to pray. I sat there, remembering the wonderful woman who had been my mother-in-law. She would remain in my heart all my life. I wanted to do something for her to show my respect—and then it came to me. I'd give up coffee, just like she'd wanted me to do. Whether it was regular, decaf, iced, or espresso, I wouldn't have coffee in any form. From that moment on, I never had coffee again.

And let me tell you, at first it was tough. I almost never get headaches, but the first four days I spent without coffee, I had the worst headaches of my life. On top of that, I was so tired I could barely keep my eyes open. But my feelings for my mother-in-law gave me the motivation I needed to hang in, and I beat the withdrawal. By the fifth day, I felt so much better—and as energized as when I'd been drinking coffee.

I haven't had a cup of coffee in more than twenty years. To this day I still love the smell of fresh coffee brewing, but now instead of thinking about how much I'd love a cup, I think of how much I loved my mother-in-law and what a special woman she was. It gives me great pleasure. It was a hard change to make, but the results were really worth it.

Change and Fashion

Don't make a change solely because it's something that everyone else is doing. A couple of years ago, the fashion trend was for women to wear their hair very short. I'm always interested in the latest styles, but I was not at all sure that cutting my hair short was a change I wanted to make. Rather than getting a drastic haircut all at once, I had it trimmed a few inches to see if I'd like it. I knew that if I did like it, I could have it cut another couple of inches again until it was short. Well, I didn't like it *at all*—I just think I look better with longer hair. My hairstyle isn't affecting my health—so why should I make a change that makes me uncomfortable? Why should any of us make a change that we don't want just because it's the fashionable thing to do, or because "they" say that's what we should be doing? I still wear long hair even though "they" say that women should cut their hair when they get older. I'm still a brunette, even though "they" say that women should lighten their hair as they get older. (And by the way, when it comes to hair changes, it really is a good idea to sample a change before doing anything drastic. I once wondered how I'd look as a blonde. Instead of dying my hair, I decided to try on some blond wigs. Let's just say that I was cured of wanting to become a blonde—ever).

Decide to Change

I like the way I look; I feel good about me. Decide to make changes that will improve how you feel about you—not because "they" say it's the way things should be done.

Even making changes that we want to make—changes that we feel *motivated* to make—is tough. So how do we navigate changes that we didn't ask for or that we don't want?

The first thing we have to decide is whether we're going to make the change. Most of the time, it's our choice. If your doctor tells you that you have to lose weight or you have to stop smoking, you can fight that change by ignoring her advice or going to a different doctor. You can decide that you're going to keep your bad habits even if it means that because of them, you'll probably die prematurely. It's your choice—you can do whatever you want. But why would anyone make a choice that shortens her life when life itself is such a gift?

I don't like to wear a seat belt. In fact, I don't know anyone who enjoys wearing one—they can be so uncomfortable. And anyone over the age of thirty-five can remember a time when we didn't *have* to wear seat belts. But now it's the law—in some states, you can be fined if the police pull you over and you're not wearing one. We've also been educated to know that we're much more likely to survive a car accident if we are wearing a seat belt. So I made the choice to wear a seat belt every time that I get into a car. I figured that I can't control whether someone runs into my car, but I can control how well protected I am at the time. Now putting on my seat belt has become as automatic for me as opening and closing the car door. I made the choice to change. Think of how often we read in the paper or see on the news that people have been seriously injured or killed in car accidents and that they *weren't* wearing seat belts. Sadly, they made their choices, too. Choosing to make positive changes—replacing bad habits with good habits—is really giving yourself a better chance at living better, longer, and happier. I want to live a long time—at least to be 150. (I used to say I wanted to live to be 120, but I've decided that's not long enough.)

Whenever possible, make the choice to have fun with change. I'd get bored taking that daily walk I talked about earlier if I didn't mix it up a little. Changing the routine is what keeps me interested. Sometimes I'll take different routes for a change of scenery. Other times, I'll walk until I see someone walking toward me in the distance. Then I'll jog until they either pass me or turn onto another street. Then I'll go back to walking. If I get bored with that, I'll change the game so that I start jogging when a white car drives by and go back to walking when a red car drives by. I've done the same thing with in-state and out-of-state license plates. They're just easy little ways that help make change more fun.

Lisa's Story

When painful or frightening changes are thrust upon us, we need to find ways to get and stay positive. Lisa Jesswein, one of my Remarkable Women, is a master of that art. The younger of identical twins, Lisa faced more than her fair share of physical challenges at a young age. Her kidneys had never properly developed, and it seemed that her condition was always changing—and never for the better. By the age of six, she had to have blood work every week to monitor her kidney function. At twelve, she was on dialysis three times a week; by sixteen, she had had her first kidney transplant; and by twenty-five, those new kidneys failed. Through it all, Lisa navigated these changes by maintaining a positive attitude and focusing on a healthy future. "I didn't waste my energy dwelling on why this had happened to me. Ultimately, *why* didn't matter. It was the way things were. Sure, I had my bad days when I felt sad and frustrated. But most of the time, I put my energy into the future. I kept a very positive attitude, believing with all my heart that things were going to *change* for me . . . and change for the better. I just knew that someday I would be healthy."

By the time her donated kidneys failed, Lisa's twin sister was able to donate one of her kidneys to her. However, doctors planned a surgery before the transplant to remove her thyroid, which wasn't working properly. Lisa embraced the plan as her ticket to the healthy life she'd always hoped for.

The plan changed when her doctor spoke to her in the recovery room following the thyroid surgery. What he told her was a terrible shock: during the surgery they had found cancer in her thyroid. The doctor tried to reassure her, saying, "If you're going to have cancer, this is the best kind to have. It's highly treatable." To Lisa, it sounded like the worst oxymoron she'd ever heard. Lisa knew how important it was to face this change with a positive attitude, but at that moment, she couldn't get one. She felt frightened, out of control, and suddenly very unsure about her future. She turned to her doctor and said, "Then you find someone who has lived through this kind of cancer to come talk to me right now."

As it happened, there was a nurse working in the hospital who had survived the kind of cancer that Lisa was facing. She came to see Lisa and reassured her that this cancer was, as the doctor had said, highly treatable. She told Lisa exactly what she could expect and the time frame for treatment that was usually involved. By the time the nurse left, Lisa was feeling much more positive. Yes, the plan had changed, but Lisa had decided that this was just a "bump in the road" that she could work through. Then, at last, she'd be able to live a healthy life and never look back. And that's exactly what she did. Lisa went through radiation therapy, was pronounced cancer-free, and had her kidney transplant. That was eleven years ago. Today Lisa is a healthy thirty-six-year-old woman with a great career and the same positive attitude about making changes.

Silver Linings

As the saying goes, every cloud really does have a silver lining. The question is whether we choose to focus on the large, threatening dark gray cloud or on the beautiful light around it. I knew a young woman named Rose whose husband, Larry, worked in sales. Larry's job required a fair amount of travel, but when he was home, they did absolutely everything together. They ate their meals together, enjoyed the same hobbies, and socialized with the same friends. One morning while her husband was away, the doorbell rang and she opened it to find Larry's boss standing there, looking very upset. He'd had a call from the hotel. Larry hadn't answered his morning wake-up call so a member of the staff went to his door, but there was still no answer. Finally, they used a passkey to get into the room. Larry—who was only forty-two years old—had died of a heart attack during the night. Of course, Rose was shocked and devastated.

It was the most difficult time in Rose's life, but the way she handled it was very inspiring. About a year after Larry's death,

I heard from a mutual friend that Rose had gone to work at an interior design company. I called to congratulate her on her new position, and we decided to meet for lunch. I asked her how her new job had come about. She said that after Larry died, she had to make herself get up and do something with her days. Their family room had needed a makeover for some time, so to occupy herself, she decided to take on the task. "When I was finished, I realized that I'd been able to do this all on my own, and I loved the way the room looked," Rose said. "I also realized that I have a talent for this kind of work."

Soon after the room was completed, Rose saw an ad for an assistant in an interior design shop and, almost on a whim, she applied for the job—and got it. She started out doing a lot of clerical work but also learned a lot about the business. Rose said that she now looked forward to getting up and going to work every day. Would she have traded in her new family room and her new job if she could have Larry back? In an instant. But that wasn't a choice that Rose was given. She had found a way to embrace change—to make the most of the choices that she was given—by building new beginnings and new opportunities one day at a time.

You don't have to wait for your world to turn upside down to make new beginnings. What are the changes that you want to make? What new opportunities are you ready to embrace to get more out of your life?

Be Proud of Your Accomplishments

Even when we've proven to ourselves that we can embrace change, it's easy to go back to doubting ourselves when the need for a change comes along. I've seen this in some people who are nearing their goal weight at Weight Watchers. They may have lost 20, 30, 50, 60, even 100 pounds or more . . . but they are afraid to go on maintenance. Maintenance is the part of the program where people who have reached their goal weight add enough food to their daily intake to stop losing weight and stay put at their goal weight. I've even seen people with less than five pounds left to lose sabotage their own weight loss so that they wouldn't have to face maintenance. They are afraid that they'll lose control and put the weight back on. I remind them that they don't have to be afraid. If they've gotten this close to their goal, they've already made a lot of great changes that will help them keep their weight off and make the maintenance plan a permanent part of their lives.

When we have doubts, it's easier if we write down all the changes we've made and then add the changes we'd still like to make now. Really look at that list, appreciate your own accomplishments, and then write at the bottom, "I will maintain a healthy weight from now on." When you see it as just one item at the end of a long list of accomplishments, you're going to feel much more secure with your ability to make the change to keep your weight off for good.

And this isn't just true of weight loss. You can do this anytime you're facing a change that is making you feel insecure or a little down. If it's a change at work, think about all the changes you've already managed from landing your first job until today. If you're moving to a new place, think about other moves you've made—from a new school to a new neighborhood or a new job, wherever—and how you were able to make moving to those new places work for you. You can do it if you believe you can do it. The more you give yourself credit for the changes you've already managed, the more confident you'll feel about your ability to handle the next ones.

Above all, be patient with yourself in the face of change. Reaching your goal—whatever that goal may be—is great, but having fun along the way is just as great. Sure, you may have setbacks along the way, but if you keep a positive attitude about the changes you're making and if you're motivated to keep moving forward, you can make change work for you. And for every change that you make, you'll find a stronger, more confident, more joyful you greeting the mirror at the beginning of each new day.

EXERCISE: It's Time for a Change!

Everyone has changes she can make to improve—or maybe even lengthen—her life. I believe there's no time like right now to begin!

1. The hardest thing about making a change is getting started. Try a little brainstorming. If you have your "Things I Don't Like about Me *That I Can Change*" list, that will work fine. If not, get a piece of paper and write down all the things that you would like to change about yourself, your lifestyle, and/or your attitude. Some of the areas you might want to consider are weight loss, fitness, finances, relaxation time (especially if you're a workaholic), or even dealing with a lost job or a difficult relationship.

2. Make sure that every change you have listed is a *single* change. If you're fifty pounds overweight and never exercise, don't write, "I want to get physically healthy." There are several changes packed into that one statement. Try something more like, "I want to start walking for thirty minutes a day, three times a week," or "I want to add a fruit or a vegetable to every meal I eat."

3. Take a look at your list and be honest with yourself about which changes you really have the motivation to make. You might know that you need to stop smoking because

nearly everyone you know, including your doctor, has told you so. But if you have absolutely no desire to quit, that is not a change you can make right now. When it comes to making lasting change, it doesn't matter what everyone else wants or thinks—*you* have to want it.

Put a star next to every change that you feel motivated to make right now. You're not writing off the other changes forever—you're just saving them for another day.

4. Ask yourself if the time is right to make each change that you've starred. If you want to start saving more money, the week before you leave for your dream vacation may not be the right time. Set yourself up for success.

5. Choose just one change from your list that you feel ready to make.

6. Now, make a plan for change. As with all plans, you've decided what you want; now decide what you're willing to give up to get it. If you want to spend more time with your family, you may have to give up working overtime (and the pay that goes with it).

7. Make a timeline for your change (remember, it takes at least four months of repeating a behavior day in and day out to change a habit) and *take action*.

8. Find ways to reward your accomplishments and learn from your mistakes.

9. Keep going and be kind to yourself. If you've got a positive attitude and find ways to keep yourself motivated, you can make a lasting change in your life. And just think how great you'll feel about yourself when you do!

10. Four months from now—when you've conquered your change—it's time to take another look at your list. You'll feel more ready and able than ever to make another

change—maybe even one that you weren't motivated to make before!

Some Great Resources

Change Your Life Now: Powerful Techniques for Positive Change by William J. Knaus

Changing for Good by James O. Prochaska

Make the Connection: Ten Steps to a Better Body and a Better Life by Bob Greene and Oprah Winfrey

Recipes for the Journey: A Cookbook and Guide to Good Health in Recovery by Kate Smith and Jenny Fox

What Do You Want to Do When You Grow Up?: Starting the Next Chapter of Your Life by Dorothy Cantor

Who Moved My Cheese? An A-Mazing Way to Deal with Change in Your Work and in Your Life by Spencer Johnson

7

A Whole Lotta Choices Goin' On

God has given us two incredible things: absolutely awesome ability and freedom of choice. The tragedy is that, for the most part, many of us have refused them both.
—Frank Donnelly

It is not our abilities that show what we really are. It is our choices.
—J. K. Rowling

There has never been another you. With no effort on your part you were born to be something very special and set apart. What you are going to do in appreciation of that gift is a decision only you can make.
—Dan Zadra

Choose your love; love your choice.
Thomas S. Monson

IN THE LAST CHAPTER, I told you the story of why I gave up drinking coffee. I do, however, still love the smell of fresh coffee brewing. On a recent trip, I stopped at a coffee bar in the airport to enjoy that wonderful aroma. Next to me, I heard a gentleman order a large hazelnut latte made with skim milk, without whipped cream or chocolate shavings, but with a dash of cinnamon. Back when I was a coffee drinker, ordering coffee was a very simple thing to do: regular or decaf in size small, medium, or large. It occurred to me that somewhere along the line, ordering coffee had gotten very involved.

As I walked past an ice cream shop in the airport, I noticed that this wasn't just a coffee phenomenon. It used to be that a good ice cream selection meant they had chocolate, vanilla, strawberry, chocolate chip, butter pecan, and maybe a flavor of the month. This one had at least twenty different flavors of ice cream, plus frozen yogurt, a variety of "mix-ins," *and* four different types of cones.

Not only is there more variety than ever before, but we can have that variety in an almost endless number of sizes. When I was growing up and I ordered a Coke, I got an eight-ounce drink. But now fast-food restaurants are selling soft drinks in kids'-size, medium, large, and *super*size (which is the size I'd become if I drank that much soda).

A World of Choices

Today we are constantly bombarded with choices. We are living in a choice explosion. And while it's great to have more options for increasing our happiness and satisfaction in life, too much of anything can be bad. Sometimes the sheer number of choices we make in a day can be overwhelming. Think about the average working woman and what she may have to consider on any given day. What will I wear? What is the first project I need to tackle at work? What will I pack for lunch? Should I go to the gym? Will I have time to pick up the dry cleaning before that late-day meeting? Should I switch to online bill-paying or write checks? A telemarketer is offering me another cell phone plan—should I switch? Should I take work home tonight? What will I do for dinner? When will I find time to do laundry? Whew! I'm tired just thinking about them all! And those are the easy choices.

We're spending so much energy on the everyday choices that we have little left to deal with the really big ones. Should I take the job offer that means I'll have to relocate? Should I get married (or move in, get divorced, remarry, etc.)? Should I take the plunge and buy a house (build a new house, refinance, sell and move into a condo, etc.)? Should we have a child (or another child)? Should I work at home? Mom can't live alone anymore—now what do we do? I'm getting tired again just writing about it.

People everywhere are getting tired of—and even over-whelmed by—choice. But the reality is that as long as we're alive, the choices are going to keep coming. It's up to us to learn how to manage all those choices so that they work *for* us instead of running us. That's where talking to the mirror can help you.

Choose to Talk to the Mirror

The first—and I think the most important—choice that I make every day is that early morning talk with the mirror. I don't believe for a minute that a good or bad day is just something that happens to me. I *choose* to have a great day. When I wake up in the morning and make my way into the bathroom, I'm not sure at first how I feel and I don't know what to expect from my day. But as I look into my mirror, I start feeling the energy coming up from my toes until it reaches my eyes as I say, *Florine, today is going to be a good one, and you can do anything you want if you want it bad enough.* I don't set myself up for failure by asking myself to do things that I know I will fail at. As I've said before, I've always wanted to be taller, but until someone invents Grow Watchers, I'm going to stay the same height. There is no point in dwelling on what I can't change. I can think about what I want to accomplish today and say, *Florine, this is going to be a great day! You can reach all your goals if you want to bad enough, so go out there and make it happen!* Some days that one talk is enough. It's inside of me— I own that feeling. Other days, when things aren't going as planned, I might have to have that talk with the mirror two or three times to keep myself convinced that it is a great day.

Now, you might say that I'm brainwashing myself. And you know what? You're right, and I highly recommend it. I brainwash myself every day into feeling good just like I used to brainwash myself every day into feeling sorry for myself and having negative thoughts.

Most unhappy people are already brainwashed. They've either brainwashed themselves into being unhappy, or they've been conditioned from an early age to view the world as a place of disappointment. People do it all the time. ("Life isn't fair. Nobody has it as hard as I do. My girlfriends make twice as much money, all the great guys are taken, my five-year-old wants to dress like Britney Spears.") On the other hand, we can brainwash ourselves into being happy. ("I am so lucky. I like what I'm going to wear today, I like my job, my family is healthy, I live in a home where I feel safe and secure.") You know, so many people are starving, homeless, critically ill . . .

we have to really count our blessings every day. Make talking to the mirror your first choice of the day. You may not be able to radically change your mood, but I promise you, if you start talking to the mirror every day, brainwashing yourself into a new, more positive mind-set, that choice alone will have a tremendous impact on everything that follows. As the author Sondra Anice Barnes said, "It's so hard when I have to, and so easy when I want to." Isn't that the truth?

Some people might call me a Pollyanna, and I guess I really am. But I also know that there are days that no matter how hard you try, you can't be happy. I've been talking to the mirror for thirty years and there are still moments when I don't like what I'm doing, when I'm not proud of myself, when I feel lousy for no good reason. On those days, you have to focus on the fact that this, too, shall pass, there will be a tomorrow, and when you wake up the next day, you'll have a new opportunity to be happy.

Realize When You Can Choose

Now that we've dealt with that first choice of the day, how are we going to cope with every one that follows? Start by asking yourself one important question, and that question may surprise you. *Do I really have a choice to make?* Sometimes we get so caught up in making choices—probably because we have so many to make—that we start trying to decide everything. We lose sight of the fact that some things aren't ours to decide. Some things *are* beyond our control, and dwelling on them is a waste of energy. Let's say, for example, that someone at work doesn't like you. You can choose to ask that person why she doesn't like you, you can choose to avoid that person, you can even choose to leave your job if that person makes you truly miserable. But you have absolutely no choice about whether or not that person chooses to like you. That is her choice. In fact, you have no choice about how others behave at all—your only choice is how you behave and how you respond to other people's behavior.

Once you've determined that you've actually got a choice to make, it's time to analyze the options. And again, it boils down to my secret of success: *decide what you really want and what you're willing to give up to get it.* There is a famous story about Jascha Heifetz, who was considered by many to be the greatest violinist of the twentieth century. A young boy who was studying the violin was awestruck when he saw Heifetz perform. Afterward, the boy had a chance to meet Heifetz and said to him, "I'd give my life to play the violin the way you do." Heifetz said, "Well, that's exactly what I did. If you're willing to give up eight hours of your life, seven days a week to practice, from the time you're young, you can play like this, too." Making choices—like living dreams—comes with a price tag.

Go for It!

Give those life-altering choices careful consideration. Keep in mind, though, that there is a fine line between taking enough time to make an informed decision and putting things off. Analyze the situation, come to a conclusion, and, for better or worse, *go for it!* Living your life doesn't require perfection—just action. And remember, you can always make changes along the way.

Like anyone else, I've had to make choices that have changed the course of my life. I chose to have a large family and build an international business. To have those things, I had to give up having lifelong friendships. I know a lot of women who have had friends for decades—since grade school, high school, or college. Making and maintaining those friendships takes nurturing, and I never had the time. I had to give up the satisfaction I could have had in being there for girlfriends and the comfort I would have taken when they'd have been there for me. But I was too busy meeting the needs of my family and my business . . . there just wasn't time for friends.

But priorities change. Those girlfriend relationships have become very important to me. My children are grown now so they don't need as much of my time. I could still spend that extra time working in my business, but I don't. I'm choosing to spend more time with girlfriends—making up for that lost time is my priority now because they enrich my life. They are so important.

Some of us become afraid of making choices. We're either afraid that we'll make a bad choice, or that by making a choice, we're permanently closing the door on another, *better* choice. So we give up our decision-making power to others. We think that if our mother or spouse or boss or friend makes the choice for us, we won't be responsible if things go wrong. There are two problems with that approach. First, leaving our choices to others is still making a choice; and second, while others make the choices, we're the ones who live with the outcome.

If you've become a passenger in your own life, it's time to get back in the driver's seat.

The habit of making choices is a lot like the habit of exercise. It's true. If you've been active all your life, you can't imagine life without exercise. But if walking from the couch to the kitchen is as far as you go, exercise will be an acquired taste. If you've been letting others call all the shots, making your own choices will *also* be an acquired taste. But like exercise, the more often you do it, the less it hurts. You'll probably even begin to enjoy it.

Like exercise, start slow and work your way up. Begin by making small decisions that are not life-altering choices. Remember, once you decide what you want, you can always make a change later. It isn't cast in stone. I once heard somebody say that the highways of life are full of flat squirrels that couldn't make up their minds. Don't end up as a flat squirrel. If you don't know where to start, start anywhere and make changes as necessary—but please just *start*.

When Choices Hurt

As your newfound desire to make your own choices becomes apparent, don't expect the former decision makers in your life to be happy about it. Making choices is power, and you're taking that power away from those who have gotten used to having it. They may not be in a hurry to give it up. Try to be sensitive to their feelings, explain your need to make your own choices, but don't let them tell you that you aren't equipped to make your own decisions. No one is better equipped to make decisions about your life than you. You're the one who gets to bask in the glory and you're the one who has to live with the consequences.

Remember, everyone makes bad choices once in a while. They may seem like good choices at the time; when we look back, however, we wonder how we could ever have made such a decision. But you know what? Good, bad, or somewhere in between . . . they're still *our* decisions. We've all heard people (and maybe some of those people are us) say things like, "My boyfriend made me so mad that I ate a whole bag of potato chips." Of course, that's just not true. Others may behave in ways that make us angry, but we decide whether or not to respond by eating or smoking or drinking. Part of making choices is taking responsibility for those choices.

If you make a bad choice, there are three positive things you can do.

First, figure out what went wrong. Maybe you needed more information before making the choice, maybe you had incorrect information, maybe you weren't honest with yourself—or maybe you couldn't have known it was a bad choice at the time.

Second, do damage control. Minimize the consequences as best as you can, whether it's by cutting your losses, changing a plan, or seeing it through. You'll have to decide (another choice!) the best course of action. And above all, don't beat yourself up over it. That's the worst thing we can do. Asking yourself over and over, "Why did I do that?" or wasting time wishing that you hadn't done it, serves no good purpose. Just get right on with doing your best to make things right.

Lastly, apply what you've learned in the future. Life is filled with experiences that turn out to be mistakes; the most productive thing to do is learn from them.

Victoria's Story

Victoria Johnson, a Remarkable Woman, used this formula and not only survived her poor choices that led to destructive habits, she turned them around to build a thriving business. Victoria knew the benefits of exercise. In fact, she made her living as a low-impact aerobics instructor, working with people who had serious weight problems. So Victoria was always the smallest woman in the room. When her weight started a steady climb up the scale, she didn't think much about it. One day, Victoria fainted right in the middle of class. When she came to, she headed straight for her doctor's office.

When her doctor asked her to step on the scale, Victoria

was shocked to see that at five three, she weighed more than 170 pounds. The doctor examined Victoria and asked her several questions, especially about her diet. It turns out that Victoria had become hypoglycemic, had high blood pressure, and her cholesterol had skyrocketed to a dangerous level. Hypoglycemia, or low blood sugar, is a condition that occurs when you don't have enough glucose in your blood to fuel your body. Victoria found out that her diet—which was very high in starches and sweets—was what had gone wrong.

Victoria went into immediate damage control mode. She learned everything she could about her condition and what changes she could make in terms of how often she ate and what she ate.

Victoria applied what she learned by eating a more balanced diet, eating smaller portions of food, and switching from eating three large meals to eating five or six minimeals each day. She also increased the intensity of her aerobic workouts and added weight training to speed up her metabolism. Within six months, Victoria had shed her excess weight and just as important, her hypoglycemia had disappeared. Today Victoria is strong, healthy, and back down to a size four.

That tale alone would make Victoria a Remarkable Woman, but her story doesn't end there. Victoria shared what she learned with the people in her aerobics classes and developed quite a following. In fact, she now helps people get fit nationwide. She is a published author, produces her own best-selling exercise videotapes, tours the country as a motivational speaker, and has even done endorsements for Nike athletic shoes. Talk about taking lemons and making lemonade! Victoria took poor choices, turned them around to become positive and healthy ones, and made them into a dream career.

But what about when you've looked at the choices you have and none of them seem very good? That depends on the choices. Your best choice may be to dig in and make the best of your situation. Other times, you've got to be prepared to make a leap of faith into the unknown.

Sheila's Story

My daughter had a friend named Sheila who married right out of college. Her husband, Danny, and she met at school and dated for about two years. They were both energetic and had a very active social life. Their relationship was great for the first five years. They worked hard during the day and played hard at night. If there was a party, you could bet they'd be there. Eventually, though, Sheila wanted to start a family. She had always loved children and, at twenty-seven, was getting bored with their nightlife. Danny made no secret of the fact that he wasn't ready to become a father or a homebody. Sheila decided to be patient and she was . . . for four more years. At thirty-one, Danny was still the life of the party, but Sheila was partied out. They began to argue about where and how often they would go out, Danny began to resent Sheila's biological clock, and she began to see him as immature—the same college kid at thirty-one that he had been at twenty-one. Sheila began making excuses not to go out, and Danny began going without her. Soon, she began to suspect that Danny wasn't always going out alone. They tried repeatedly to talk it out, but they always ended up arguing. Finally, after a very heated discussion, Danny told her that he never wanted to have children, and Sheila knew that he meant it.

Sheila realized at that moment that she had a choice to make. She either had to give up the idea of having children or give up Danny and hope that she would meet someone else to spend her life with—someone who wanted a family. She couldn't imagine life without children, but she also couldn't imagine life without Danny. Sheila was honest enough with herself to know that she had outgrown Danny—it was unlikely that he would ever tire of going to one party after another. But she couldn't imagine life on her own. She'd gone from her parents' house to college to her husband's house. And what if that someone else *wasn't* out there?

A few months later, Sheila made her choice. She moved out of the apartment that Danny and she had shared; they divorced soon after. I knew she'd had a very difficult time making that decision and asked her why she finally decided to make the break. Sheila said, "I realized that you can be alone—even when you're with someone. I didn't want to be someone who sacrificed her dreams because she was too afraid to be on her own." Ironically, Sheila did meet Mr. Right—at her college reunion. ("Right ballpark, wrong seat!" she now says of her first marriage.) When they're not at work, you can usually find them at home with their two sons and one golden retriever.

The bottom line is that when you're faced with hard choices—when none of the options feel very good—you've got to make the best choice you can with the information you have, remember that there is a tomorrow, and have faith that brighter days will come. Sheila could have decided not to have children, and, if she could have learned to live with that, she might have saved her marriage. But she realized that having a family was the only right choice for her, so the answer for her became clear.

If you find yourself struggling with a choice, talk it over with your mirror. Remember, you are your own best friend. The more you talk to the mirror, the more honest you become with yourself. That's the path that will help you to work through the choices you're making now *and* to work through the baggage of past choices you've carried around for a long time.

And remember, make your choices based on what's good

for you—not on what is best for somebody else or what somebody else tells you is best. Take in all the information, ask yourself how you feel about the options, and make the best choice for *you*.

EXERCISE: The Anatomy of Smart Decision Making

The next time you're faced with a difficult choice, follow these step-by-step instructions to take a good hard look at your options. While there is no way to know for certain that you'll make the best choice, you *will* know you made the best decision you could with the information you had at the time. And that's all that any of us can expect of ourselves.

1. Think about the decision that you have to make and start brainstorming your options. Don't be satisfied with just looking at the obvious choices. Be creative—even if an option seems completely impractical, it will get your creative juices flowing. Write them all down on paper.

2. Now it's time to take a closer look. For each option, list the possible consequences—good and bad. This step can be time-consuming, but it's important to really do your homework so that you uncover all the possible consequences. Start with the options that at least on the surface seem the most practical.

3. Once you've looked at the practical options, take a look at your more creative ideas. Are they really so far-fetched . . . or just a completely new approach? Sometimes a fresh start or an unexpected response is exactly what we need when we have a difficult choice to make. Or maybe they are impractical on the whole but have a few elements that you can use to make your other options better.

4. Look at all the consequences and ask yourself, "When I look at all the benefits versus the risks, what is the best choice for me?" Be honest with yourself about what you really are prepared to do and what you're not prepared to do.

5. Make a choice and go for it! If it turns out to be a good choice, you have yourself to thank. If it turns out to be a not-so-good choice, learn from what went wrong, dust yourself off, and make a new choice!

Some Great Resources

Body Revival: Lose Weight, Feel Great, and Pump Up Your Faith by Victoria Johnson

Choices: Creating Happiness by Breaking Free from Your Past by Andrea J. Moses

Decision Traps: Ten Barriers to Brilliant Decision-Making and How to Overcome Them by J. Edward Russo

How Good People Make Tough Choices: Resolving the Dilemmas of Ethical Living by Rushworth M. Kidder

Smart Choices: A Practical Guide to Making Better Decisions by John S. Hammond

The Thinker's Toolkit: 14 Powerful Techniques for Problem Solving by Morgan D. Jones

Wisdom for Earthlings: How to Make Better Choices and Take Action in Your Life and in Your Work by John E. Newman

8

How to Beat the Blues

I like living. I have sometimes been wildly,
despairingly, acutely miserable, racked with sorrow,
but through it all I still know quite certainly that
just to be alive *is a grand thing.*
—Agatha Christie

Better to lose count while naming your blessings then
to lose your blessings to counting your troubles.
—Maltbie D. Babcock

The talent for being happy is appreciating what
you have instead of what you don't have.
—Woody Allen

Happiness is a conscious choice, not an automatic response.
—Mildred Barthel

S OME MORNINGS I BOUND out of bed, tell myself it's going to be a great day, and jump right into it. Other mornings— maybe it's raining outside or I didn't get enough sleep—I feel as if there really is a wrong side of the bed, and it's the side I got up on. I'm standing at the mirror for five minutes, *convincing* myself that it's going to be a great day. But I beat those blues and that is what's important. You can beat them, too, but it takes practice, talking to that mirror every day.

Would you like to know my very best secret for beating the blues? I decide not to have them in the first place. That's right— I get up every morning, head straight for my mirror, and say, *Good morning, Florine! This is going to be a great day!* Sound simple? In a way it is. It's a lifestyle choice, just like exercising every day is a lifestyle choice. Still sound simple? Maybe not, because those of us who exercise every day (and those of us who don't) know that it's not always easy to stay committed. Some days we wake up ready to go, but other days, it takes real determination to get moving. Starting the day feeling happy works in exactly the same way.

Like exercise, choosing to be happy becomes a habit. The more you do it, the more it becomes a natural way to start your day, like brushing your teeth or getting that first cup of coffee. You own it, it becomes part of you . . . but little by little, this habit can change the way you view and live your life.

Having read my story, you know that I didn't start out life as a very happy person or thinking that I could change my life. I didn't think I controlled much of anything—from my mood to my weight. It was a long process of transforming the messages I was sending myself from "I can't" to "I can." But it was worth it, because in the process, I transformed myself into the person I am today.

Decide to Believe in Good Things

Now, I know that I'm a lucky person. I also know that I work very hard at being lucky. I *decide* to believe that all good things will come my way. I am genuinely surprised when things go wrong or something bad happens. And lucky things happen to me. If I'm waiting for an overbooked flight and I'm fifth on the waiting list for tickets, I believe that five tickets will be available and most of the time, there are at least five tickets. I'm actually surprised if I don't make that flight.

Too many people walk around expecting bad things to happen. Out of all the possible scenarios, they expect the worst outcome. What does that solve? Where does that get you? It doesn't make you feel any better even if the worst *does* happen—it saps the joy out of the "present" we talked about in chapter 2, and sometimes it actually sets you up for a negative outcome.

For years, I played tennis with a woman who is ten years younger than I am. We were pretty competitive, and most of the time, it seemed like our scores were tied. She'd win a game, I'd win the next one, and so on and so on, for about forty-five minutes. Then inevitably, she'd say, "I know you're going to win this last game, Florine, because you have more energy than I do." Inevitably, I'd win . . . and I mean *every* time. But the truth was that I wasn't beating her. She was beating herself. I wasn't that much more energetic or skilled than she was. If I had been, our scores wouldn't be so close after each game. But for whatever reason, she decided she wasn't going to win that last set and it threw off her performance ever so slightly. When she let go of that bit of confidence, she actually gave me the edge.

Another mistake that people make is when they lose that positive momentum the minute things go wrong. It's easy to keep smiling when everything is going your way, but to really benefit, you've got to stay positive when things *aren't* going your way. Remember, it's not over till it's over.

I know a woman named Julie. When her day suddenly goes downhill, she responds by saying in a loud southern drawl, "Somethin' good is gonna to happen to me *today*!" It gives her coworkers a chuckle (partly because Julie isn't even southern) and puts the smile back on her face, and she says something good usually *does* happen to her that same day.

Julie knows it doesn't have to be a big something that happens. There is an old proverb that says: write the bad things that happen to you in sand, but write the good things that happen to you on a piece of marble. Remember and focus on all the little good things that happen in a day.

Our Night at the Theater

I may not use Julie's southern drawl, but that same positive attitude works for me. I recently went to a theater in New York where I had reserved tickets, but for some reason they had no record of the reservation. I could have gotten very upset, but that wasn't going to help anything. Instead, I regrouped, mentally pushing away my disappointment so that I could regain my positive attitude. I explained to the man at the box office that I'd come all the way from Detroit and that I loved the theater (especially this play) and asked if there was any way he could help me. He gestured to a line of people and explained that sometimes people turned in tickets at the last minute and I was welcome to wait to see if that happened. I thanked the man very much and got in line.

About three minutes before the show started, the person in the booth told the first person in line, "Sorry, it doesn't look as though there are any tickets being turned back in." The first person in line repeated it to the person behind her and so on. All it took was one negative message and everyone started leaving. Not me. With about a minute to go, nearly twenty people had left and I was the only one left in line. I just knew there were tickets. The man I'd talked to earlier saw me and said, "I guess you didn't get tickets." I said I hadn't and that I felt really bad about missing the show, but I knew he'd have helped me if he could. I thanked him and turned to go. Just then, he said, "Wait! Someone turned in their tickets after all!" They were front-row center seats. Now maybe someone did just turn them in or maybe they were house seats kept in reserve . . . but I got the seats. There were twenty people in front of me who could have gotten those tickets instead of me. I got them because I stayed positive—when I encountered the obstacle *and* when I asked for help. I thanked the man again on my way out and told him how he'd brightened my day. A pat on the back, a reward of a smile, and a kind word is our lifeblood—we all need to get them and we all need to give them. (By the way, the show was terrific!)

Except for life's obvious victories and tragedies, it's really left to each of us to decide whether we're going to put a positive or a negative spin on what we experience. The old question "Is your glass half empty or half full?" isn't a measure of the glass but a measure of your feelings about life.

Put a Positive Spin on It

When you have a task that you're not looking forward to completing, you can put it off, but it's in the back of your mind, bringing you down a little at a time. The other choice is to set a time on your agenda to complete that task and put a positive spin on doing it.

One of the tasks I like the least is reading dry material. As a board member for several charities, I have to read everything from annual reports to strategic plans. One of the boards I sit on—and a cause that is very close to my heart—is the March of Dimes. When my agenda tells me it's time to do some reading for them, I sit down and tell myself, *Florine, you know you have to read this so you can talk intelligently at the next meeting. You may have to do a little reading that you don't like, but just think, in return you may help save more babies from birth defects.* That positive spin makes the thought of all that reading, and the reading itself, a lot easier to take.

Besides making our daily tasks easier, putting a positive spin on things can really impact the way in which we see ourselves. For example, we all sometimes forget what we were just thinking about. I might respond to that by thinking, *Florine, you must be getting old.* If I do, in addition to losing my train of thought, I'm going to feel old and maybe even a little less capable. Or, I could respond by thinking, *I've got so much going on, that thought just got lost!* Now I'm attributing it to this full, wonderful life I'm leading. Which response is going to make me feel better? Which response is going to give me a more positive outlook? Can those feelings and outlooks change the way I act over time? You bet they can! And they can change the way others act toward me, too. *People react positively to positive people.*

Every single one of us on this earth is a salesperson. Think of Julie and her coworkers. When things start to go wrong, she could walk around that office like a sourpuss, darkening the mood of everyone around her. Instead, she uses humor to brighten the moment. Julie is selling smiles. And because of that, don't you think her coworkers will be happier to be around her *and* more likely to help her out when she needs it? Of course! So think about what you're selling to people. Are you selling joy, hope, a positive attitude? Or are you selling bitterness, martyrdom, boredom, despair? Because whatever you're selling . . . that's what you're going to get back.

Our attitude affects those around us every day, and their attitudes have the power to affect us. If you're with a coworker and you're both feeling negative about your office or your boss, steer clear of that subject. Otherwise, you'll feed into each other's negativity and compound your pessimistic outlooks. Instead, gravitate to people who can compound happiness in the work you're doing. The day will go faster, you'll do quality work, and you'll just plain feel better. If you can't find joy in your work, no matter how hard you try, it's time for a change.

Jackie's and Rebecca's Stories

Sometimes choosing to be happy can take you beyond the little wins like making an overbooked flight, a tennis match, getting tickets for a show, or a good day at the office. Sometimes it has the power to change your life.

Jackie Waldman, a woman I interviewed for my *Remarkable Woman* radio show, was always a real dynamo. By the age of forty, she was at the top of the corporate ladder and living a successful life. Then she was stricken with multiple sclerosis. At first, she was devastated—anyone would be. She became very negative and depressed about her illness. The worse her attitude became, the worse her symptoms became. One day she decided she'd had enough. Jackie put every ounce of positive energy she had into being the best she could be. She exercised and ate well, and she did it all with the same enthusiasm that had made her a professional success. Gradually, her symptoms started to lessen. Now her MS is in remission, and she's back to doing the work she loves. Jackie says she knows the mind/body connection exists and that her remission wouldn't have been possible if she hadn't conquered her negative attitude first.

Making the choice to stay positive can not only change your life in profound ways, but it can also impact the lives of those around you. Rebecca grew up in Ohio during the 1940s in a family of modest means. More than anything, Rebecca wanted to be a doctor but knew she had little chance. Few women in those days became physicians, and her family could never have afforded medical school. Rebecca could have become very negative, even bitter. Instead, she worked hard saving money to achieve something she *could* have—Rebecca decided to become a veterinarian instead of a physician. It seemed like a challenging but more attainable goal. She studied every spare moment she got. Not long after she took the veterinarian school entrance exams, she got a call from a member of the board who had reviewed her scores. Rebecca had scored very high—so high that the board had recommended her for a scholarship to medical school.

Rebecca became a doctor in one of Pennsylvania's most rural areas. She drove her truck to make house calls, treating people who otherwise might not have gotten the care they needed. Rebecca married, and eight months into her first pregnancy, while driving in the middle of nowhere she went into labor. She climbed into the back of her truck and delivered her own twin daughters. Today Rebecca is retired, but her two daughters—who also became doctors—continue to serve many of the same families that Rebecca cared for.

What would have happened if Rebecca had just felt sorry for herself? What if she hadn't tried her best because it didn't look as though she could have what she wanted most? How many lives did Rebecca change with her decision to study hard, to stay positive, and to do her best? Certainly she changed her own life and those of her daughters, but she also changed the lives—maybe even *saved* the lives—of countless patients.

Choose to Love the Moment

It's important to note that although staying positive can change your life for the better, you can't control everything. Sometimes things aren't going to turn out the way you hoped they would. But staying positive will give you some control, even in situations where you may otherwise feel powerless.

I recall a story about an elderly woman who hadn't been well for a number of years. Her husband, who had always taken care of her, had died, and she had no choice but to enter a nursing home. Certainly it wasn't what she wanted . . . what she wanted was the comforting home she'd known for so long and the beautiful garden outside it. But it just wasn't possible anymore. She sat patiently in the waiting area while her room was prepared. It was a long wait, and the aide who came to show her to her room apologized for the delay. "I'm sorry this took so long," she said. "We were putting new eyelet curtains in your room. I know the room is small, but the curtains will cheer it up a little." The woman replied, "I love it." The aide was confused by this. "But, ma'am, you haven't even seen the room yet." "It doesn't matter," said the woman. "I've already decided that I'm going to love it. I've learned over the years that we can't always choose what happens to us, but we can choose how we feel about it. And I'm choosing to love it."

A positive attitude can empower you even in situations that you can't change—and it certainly makes those situations easier to bear. The woman in the story couldn't choose the moment she was in, but she could (and did) choose to love the moment.

You can make a plan to keep the blues away. First, make a conscious choice to be happy. Before you go to bed tonight, write yourself a note and tape it to your bathroom mirror so you'll see it as soon as you get up. The note should say, "This is going to be a great day!" Second, talk to the mirror about your plans for the day and how lucky you are to have them. Third, set aside that hour to do things and talk to people that bring you joy (see chapters 2 and 3). Finally, add these reminders to your daily agenda: "Smile and say hello to everyone you know—and everyone you don't." "Look for the good in today's tasks." "Live in the moment and love the moment you're in." And at the bottom, it wouldn't hurt to include "Somethin' good is gonna happen to me today!"

SELF-TEST: Okay, You've Fallen . . .
Are You Ready to Get Up?

No matter how good we get at being positive, every now and then a bad day will knock us down. When that happens, I remind myself that this, too, shall pass and there is a tomorrow. And sooner or later, we all experience serious loss (of a job, a marriage, a loved one, our health, etc.) that requires time to grieve. Take that time. But if afterward, you still can't get back on your feet, you may be suffering from depression. Take the test below to find out.

For the last two weeks or more, have you:

Felt overwhelmed by a sense of sadness or
    hopelessness?   Yes   No

Lost your appetite?   Yes   No

Wanted to eat all the time, even when
    you're not hungry?   Yes   No

Had little or no energy?	Yes	No
Had trouble falling asleep or staying asleep?	Yes	No
Been sleeping too much or been tired all the time?	Yes	No
Been feeling like a failure or like you let your loved ones down?	Yes	No
Had trouble concentrating on everyday tasks or activities?	Yes	No
Had little interest in things you usually enjoy?	Yes	No
Thought that your life is worthless or wished your life was over?	Yes	No

If you answered yes to five or more of the above questions, you *may* be suffering from depression. Please reach out to a family member, friend, counselor, doctor, minister, priest, or rabbi. Get it all out and get it into perspective. Once you get the help you need, you can return to that friend in the mirror.

Everyone can benefit from therapy at some point in her life. It's nothing to be embarrassed about. When my sister died, I found that my grieving was long and deep. No matter how hard I tried, I couldn't get over my feelings of loss. I was having feelings that interfered with my ability to live my life, so I saw a therapist who enabled me to work through it. I think of those sessions as a gift I gave myself and help that my sister would want me to have. So if you think you might be suffering from depression, get help; but if it's just the blues, make a commitment to making each day brighter by starting it with a talk to your friend in the mirror.

Some Great Resources

Defeating Depression and Beating the Blues: A Holistic, Nutritional and Spiritual Approach by Patricia Webb

Happiness Is Free: And It's Easier Than You Think! by Hale Dwoskin and Lester Levenson

Help Yourself Get the Happiness Habit: How You Can Choose Your Steps to a Happy Life by Christine Webber

How We Choose to Be Happy: The 9 Choices of Extremely Happy People, Their Secrets, Their Stories by Rick Foster and Greg Hicks

The Power of Positive Thinking by Norman Vincent Peale

When Am I Going to Be Happy?: How to Break the Emotional Bad Habits That Make You Miserable by Penelope Russianoff

You Can Choose to Be Happy: "Rise Above" Anxiety, Anger, and Depression by Tom Stevens

9

TAKE THE DISTRESS OUT OF STRESS

Worry is like a rocking chair; it gives you something
to do but it doesn't get you anywhere.
—EVAN ESAR

Find what things you can have some control over,
and come up with creative ways to take control.
—DR. PAUL ROSCH

They say stress is a killer. But I think no stress *is equally*
deadly. If your days just seem to slip by without any
highs or lows, without some anxieties and pulse-quickening
occurrences, you may not be really living.
—HELEN HAYES

W E COMPLAIN ABOUT IT, get massages for it, overeat
because of it, we even make ourselves sick with it . . .

but without it, very little would get done. It's called stress. We talked briefly in chapter 2 about how stress can take the joy out of our days. In this chapter, I'm going to share the bag of tricks that I use to make the most of positive stress and, even more important, take the distress out of negative stress.

We almost always think of stress as bad, but like many things in life, stress has two sides. Positive stress—the good stuff—is the adrenaline that goes through your system because you're excited about taking a trip, working to meet the deadline on a project you care about, planning your wedding, expecting a child, or becoming a grandmother for the first time. They're all stressful things, but it's *good* stress. Positive stress is the energy that makes some of the best things in life happen.

Everybody has stress, but it's what you make of your stress that counts. Negative thoughts or feelings can create negative stress in almost any situation. Just getting up in the morning when you want to stay in bed can be stressful in a negative way. Exercising when you'd rather be doing something else can be stressful. Going to work when you'd rather be visiting with a friend or family member can be stressful. Even going shopping can be stressful—it really depends on how you look at it.

That is why talking to the mirror is so important. When I start my day in front of the mirror, giving myself positive messages and getting into a positive mind-set, it's really my way of stopping negative stress before it starts. If I have lots of positive thoughts, I can make my energy—my *positive* stress— work for me.

People always ask me how I manage to get so much done. It's because I see all the things that I have to do as a gift instead of a burden. If I woke up resenting the day ahead of me, it would just slow me down. I really do believe that God isn't going to give me more than I can handle. Apparently, I'm one of the lucky ones that God thinks can handle quite a bit. It's because my life is full that it's so enriched. I get to experience so much more because I do so much more. So every morning, I wake up and think, *I am so lucky that I get to do all these things today.* I think about the people who wake up with nothing to do and nowhere to go. I think of myself as lucky because I have eight or nine or ten things to do today. You can give yourself the same kind of positive, life-enriching messages.

Of course, some negative stress is bound to happen, so I have my own bag of tricks to keep that stress as minimal as possible. They're strategies that really work for me, and I'll bet they'll work for you, too.

Get Organized

The first trick that I use to prevent negative stress is getting organized. This is some of the oldest and best advice in the world. In fact, the Chinese have practiced the art of placement—called feng shui—for more than six thousand years. Feng shui is based on the idea that our home and business surroundings can be placed and organized to promote balance, efficiency, comfort, and harmony in our lives. A lack of organization and proper placement can, according to feng shui, be a source of stress and discomfort. Just think about the last time you frantically searched for a pen and couldn't find it because you misplaced it or someone else took it. It is so frustrating and stressful (not to mention a little embarrassing) when you want to get important information over the phone and find yourself without the means to write it down.

I try hard to make a place for everything and keep everything in its place. I keep the kinds of pens and pencils that I like to use arranged in coffee mugs. The mugs I choose always have funny sayings or pictures on them to make me smile (another de-stressor). I keep a collection of them in my office, by my phone at home, wherever I might need a pen or pencil. I keep erasers handy, too. Making a mistake (and we all make mistakes) is even more stressful when you can't find the tools you need to correct it. I also keep tablets and notepads easily within reach. I even keep an extra makeup bag in my desk so that I'm prepared to freshen up for a late-day or evening meeting. People always take pens and pencils from my desk (by mistake, of course), so whenever I see writing supplies on sale, I make sure to buy a bunch of them. Then once a week I make sure that all my supplies are in place. Knowing that I have what I need on hand just makes everyday life at the office a little less stressful for me.

At home I do the same thing. I have a cabinet with little hooks on the inside where I keep all my important keys. They're coded with nail polish so that I can easily find the one that I want. Yes, it took a little time to organize them that way, but not nearly as long as it takes to search the house every time I need a key. I keep an extra set of keys to my office and car in a place where I can easily get to them so if I lock myself out, it's no problem. My neighbor also keeps an extra key to my house in case of an emergency. Everyone in my household knows—including me—that if one of us takes a key, we need to put it back where it belongs. Most of the time, this system really works.

These may sound like small things, but organizing your workplace and your home can alleviate a lot of life's little stressors, and in time, little stressors add up to big stress.

Remember Your Agenda

My bag of tricks for reducing stress also includes my daily agenda. In chapter 2, I shared with you that keeping an agenda helps me finish my work in time to do more of the things I enjoy doing. It's also a powerful way to take the distress out of stress because it allows me to plan for my day. Surprises are great when it comes to parties, but not so great when it comes to daily living. The more prepared I am, the less negative stress I'm likely to have.

To set up your own agenda—or to make sure that you're getting the most out of the agenda you already use—start making a list of all the things that are important to you. My agenda has everything from business meetings to hair appointments to visits with my mother. If it's going to take time out of your day and it's something you have to do, that item should be included on your agenda. If you need to go shopping for a new outfit to wear on a special occasion, schedule it. That way you won't find yourself standing in front of your clothes closet on the day of the event, frantically trying to put together an outfit from clothes that don't fit properly or aren't in fashion or aren't comfortable or you just don't like. If you need to buy school supplies for your kids, schedule it. Planning to buy those supplies in advance will prevent the stress you'll feel when you rush to the store two days before school starts and you have to choose from the leftovers that nobody wanted. These are the kinds of stressful situations that we have the power to prevent.

Your six-month agenda should also include the appointments that are important to your health. Take ten minutes out of one day to schedule your next dental exam, your yearly physical, your pap smear, mammogram, and any other health screening you may need. It's stressful knowing that we're past due for that annual trip to the gynecologist. We stress over the exam itself *and* over what the doctor may find wrong with us. Schedule the appointments, make peace with the small amount of stress involved with the exams, and spare yourself the much bigger stress you'll feel from putting off those exams and wondering if you're healthy. Getting into the habit of regular health screenings takes time and effort, so talk to the mirror for reinforcement. Remind yourself why it's important to make and *keep* these appointments. By the time the first six months of your agenda have passed, you'll have added another healthy habit that will help you live better and may even help you live longer.

Of course, you also want to make sure your agenda includes the priorities you set for yourself in chapter 2 to get more joy out of each day. Schedule that daily hour of time for yourself. If you want to spend more time with family or friends, schedule that, too. In other words, schedule all the things you *have* to do and all the things you *want* to do. Schedule regular haircuts, massages, manicures, or pedicures—whatever will make you feel more confident and relaxed. I used to feel that activities like those were extravagances. I felt a little guilty when I added them to my agenda. I came to realize that they're really therapy for my negative stress—they help me relax and revitalize. They're as necessary to my well-being as eating right, exercising, and getting enough sleep. When I'm *de*-stressed, I'm in the best mental and emotional shape I can be to accomplish my goals and make my dreams happen. Being de-stressed helps me to be the best I can be for me *and* for those around me.

As you're scheduling your agenda, don't schedule appointments or activities too close together. If I'm sitting in one meeting, looking at my watch and thinking that I'm going to be late for my next meeting, I'll start to feel stressed. Then when I realize that I haven't been giving the people that I'm meeting with my full attention, I feel even more stressed.

Meetings and appointments almost always take longer than we think they will, so add a little extra time in your agenda between them. If you think your 1 P.M. meeting will take an hour and the travel time to the next meeting is a half hour, don't schedule your next meeting at 2:30 P.M. That assumes that everything will go according to plan—and just how often does that happen? Put at least an extra half hour in between the two. So what if you have to wait fifteen minutes for your 3 P.M. appointment? Spend the time reviewing what you plan to discuss, return a call on your cell phone, or thumb through a magazine. All those things are a lot less stressful than frantically rushing to make an appointment, having to apologize for being late, and feeling uncomfortable during the entire meeting.

Once your six-month agenda is in place, it's best if you forget about most of it. If I thought about everything that I have scheduled for the next six months, I'd be so overwhelmed by all the things I have to do that I wouldn't be able to do anything. So relax—just look at the things you'll be doing today and tomorrow and enjoy making the most of them *one at a time.*

Think of it this way. A few months ago, there was a fairly violent windstorm that left large and small branches all over the ground around my house, so I called a landscaping company to clean up the mess. I have to admit, though, that I had my doubts when I saw the slight stature of the elderly man they sent. *Is he going to be up to the job?* I wondered. I was working at home that morning (on this book, in fact!) and could see him at work from my window. It was a little overwhelming when I looked at the branches scattered everywhere. But the man didn't look like he was giving those branches any thought at all. He'd lift a load that he could carry comfortably and then patiently move it to the bed of his truck. He made the trip over and over until he had moved every single branch. It struck me that I was seeing the singer Lena Horne's philosophy in action: "It isn't the load that breaks you; it's the way that you carry it." You'll get a lot more done with a lot less stress if you stay focused on the task at hand instead of all that lies ahead. When I'm hiking a hill on one of my walks, I know that if I look up to the top of that hill, it's going to be overwhelming. Instead I concentrate on looking just in front of me, focusing on one step at a time as I climb that hill. Then when I reach the peak, I stop long enough to look back down over the distance I climbed and I feel so proud of myself for having made it to the top.

That's why I keep only a week's worth of agenda in my purse and, whenever possible, really look at only one day in advance. I take it out the afternoon or evening before to analyze what I can do to make the upcoming day run smoother and better. Part of that analysis includes figuring out what I should wear and laying it out in advance. Now that may sound frivolous but it's not. It's another way of stopping negative stress before it starts.

Most of my days are busy from morning through evening. If I dressed business casual for a morning meeting—where it was very appropriate—but had the same outfit on at an evening event where everyone else was wearing formal attire, I'd feel very uncomfortable. Likewise, if I walked in dressed to the nines and everyone else was wearing business casual, I'd feel out of place. Being over- or underdressed is stressful. To avoid this, I look at my agenda and think about whether the same outfit will work for the entire day. I might need to make time to come home and change; if there isn't enough time for that, I may need to take a second set of clothes to the office or maybe just accessories to dress one outfit up or down. It's worth it to take those few moments the day before to make sure that something as simple as what I'm going to wear doesn't become a major stressor.

And you know what? I've learned to always wear clothes I really like and feel good in to important events. It's one less thing I have to think about when I'm trying to make a good impression. When I look in the mirror and feel good about what I'm wearing, it's that much easier to say to myself with confidence, *Florine, this is going to be a great event! You can do anything you want if you want to do it bad enough!*

Above all, make sure that your agenda serves you and not the other way around. It's easy to get into ruts. Let's say that you always go to the supermarket on Thursdays because that's always been the most convenient day for you. Then your schedule changes so that it's more convenient to make your weekly supermarket trip on Tuesday . . . but there you are, still trying to force the trip into Thursday because that's the way it's always been. Before you know it, you're stressed out over a little thing like groceries. Remember, *if you always do what you've always done, you'll always get what you always got.* Be flexible, be adaptable, and you'll find your negative stress level plummet.

A final note on using agendas to de-stress: accept that your agenda is not the Ten Commandments or the Rosetta stone. Agendas aren't made to be cast in stone. Your negative stress level will be lower if you learn to take the changes you have to make to your plans in stride. All you can do is adjust your agenda based on what you think needs to be done the most and what you can fit into your schedule. With the hectic lifestyles we lead today, there will be times when postponements and even cancellations can't be helped.

You have to take control of what you can, make peace with what you can't control or fix, and, oh yes, stop worrying in advance about what may or may not change in the future.

Learn to Manage Worry

While it's impossible to stop worrying altogether—worrying is part of being human—learning to *manage* worry is a great way to reduce our stress. There is an old saying: "Worrying about something that may never happen is like paying interest on money that you may never borrow." To my knowledge, no catastrophe has ever been prevented simply by worrying about it in advance. The only thing that worrying about the future does is suck the joy right out of the present.

I know that this advice is much easier to give than it is to take. I have to constantly work at managing worry in my own life. For instance, when I know that one of my kids and their family are on a plane, I worry. In fact, I could easily spend the entire time they're in the air worrying about their safety. While it's normal for a mother to worry about her children, in this case, worrying doesn't solve anything. I have no control over the safety of their flight. So I head to the mirror for a talk. I say to myself, *Florine, there is no good reason to worry. Flying is much safer than traveling by car, the weather is good, and security at airports is at an all-time high. Do something productive to pass the time—something you've been meaning to do but just haven't gotten around to. By the time you're done, the kids will call you from their cell phone to tell you everything is fine. If they haven't called, you have their number—you can call them. Besides, worrying won't help them or you. Now get to work and think about something else. The time will pass quickly.* I force myself to get busy working on something productive and before I know it, the time has passed and they've landed safely.

Keep Life in Perspective

Part of worry management—and one of my best strategies to prevent negative stress—is keeping life in perspective. Sometimes we focus our attention and energy on one particular event—meeting that special someone, having children, getting a certain job, or building a new house are good examples. We become obsessed, worrying about getting what we want and thinking that getting the one person or thing we're yearning for is what our life is all about. Well, I'm here to tell you none of that is what life is all about. Life is about *how you feel* about life. It's about being happy, being kind, being happy, being responsible, and—did I mention—being happy? If today turns out to be your last day on earth and someone in the hereafter asks you, "What was your life like?" and you can answer, "I had happiness and love in my life, and I gave some of that happiness and love back to others," that's the best that you (or anyone else) can hope for. Being happy is the stuff of a wonderful life. So don't bank all your energy and long-term happiness on realizing one dream. That's just setting yourself up for long-term stress and disappointment.

Now that I've shared my bag of tricks for minimizing negative stress, I have to admit that some negative stress will work its way into your mind and spirit no matter how hard you try to prevent it. You're organized, you've got your agenda working for you, you're prepared, and then your best-laid plans go wrong.

You might make a mistake, forget something you were supposed to do, not know the answer to an important question, or say something that you wish you hadn't said. For the rest of the day, you find yourself dwelling and feeling worse and worse about what happened. The sooner you can short-circuit that negative stress, the better.

The most important stress "first-aid" is that you keep your cool. Go to the mirror and talk yourself down. I start those talks by saying something like, *Florine, is it going to help anything to get upset (lose your temper, cry, etc.)? The problem will still be there, but if you lose your cool it will be that much harder to fix. You need to stay calm so that you can think clearly and get people around you to help you find a solution. Now take a deep breath, go back in there, and stay positive.*

Sometimes it's good to remind ourselves that no one is perfect. If you don't know the answer to someone's question, it's not the end of the world. There is absolutely nothing wrong with saying, "I don't know . . . but I'll find out," and getting back to him with the answer. In fact, I respect someone more who admits he doesn't know an answer than someone who gives me incorrect information because he's guessing—especially when I'm asking for directions.

When just reminding myself that I'm not perfect isn't enough to put stressful feelings into perspective, I'll try writing down the things that are bothering me. I usually figure out that I've blown some things way out of proportion as soon as I read them. The things that remain—things that I haven't blown out of proportion—I do something about. I make a plan like the one that we talked about in chapter 5. I decide what I'm going to do, give my plan a time frame, and take action. Then I revisit how I'm progressing and evaluate whether I need to make changes to the plan as I go along. If the plan doesn't work out, that's okay—I make another plan, and another and another, if necessary, until I achieve the results I need to feel better about the situation.

When Crises Happen

We're the most vulnerable to negative stress in an emergency. Maybe you get a call from someone telling you that your parent has been in an accident or your child has fallen. In that case, you know you're going to respond—that's a given—but you have choices about *how* you'll respond to the crisis. Everyone needs someone she can count on in times of stress and crisis. You can help de-stress or you can add more stress in any situation. The way you respond in a crisis is your choice. Calming and centering yourself only takes a moment, but it can make a big difference in how things turn out for your loved one and you.

You may not have time to stand in front of your mirror at home. Maybe you're talking to your makeup mirror in a waiting room—or maybe you don't even have a mirror. You can still give yourself the positive messages that you need no matter where you are.

I'd say something to myself like, *Florine, take a deep breath. Slow down. Someone you love is in trouble. What can you do? You can be there for her and handle the situation in a positive manner. Don't make yourself so stressed and crazy that you aren't any good in this situation—that won't help anyone. After the crisis is over, you can have a good cry if you want to. The only way that you can help now is to get all the information you can and be calm. They need you to be calm and give whatever help you can.*

Then I respond in the most calm and positive way I can, and when the crisis is over, I adjust my agenda even further to give myself the time I need to recover. That includes having the good cry I promised myself to let it all out, taking a long walk to work out the tension in my body, making a fabulous meal for my family . . . or whatever is going to make me feel better.

Take Time to Recover

I can't emphasize enough the importance of regularly taking the time you need to recover from negative stress. I learned this lesson the hard way. By the time I was eighteen years old, I was married, had a child, had moved to another part of the country where I had no family, and was already realizing that my marriage had been a mistake. The stress was so bad that I started to have panic attacks. I'd start feeling like I couldn't breathe and sharp pains would shoot up my arms. I thought I was dying.

The attacks eventually got so bad that I didn't want to leave the house. When I did, I'd take one of those little bottles of alcohol that you get on airplanes to drink in case I had an attack.

Finally, I confided in my doctor about the attacks. He gave me medication to relieve the anxiety for the short term, but he also taught me my first stress-recovery tool. He told me that because of the stress I was under, my breathing was becoming fast and shallow. I was hyperventilating, which brought on and fueled the panic attacks. He suggested that when the attacks started coming on, I breathe into a paper bag to stop hyper-ventilating. I carried one around in my purse all the time—it was a much better idea that resorting to alcohol in the middle of the day. When I saw how well the paper bag worked, I real-ized that I had to start actively dealing with the negative feelings I was having. I had to face my problem head-on and find a solution that I could live with. I started building more and more ways to treat stress and most of them I use to this day.

I thought about how breathing the wrong way brought on my panic attacks, so I reasoned that breathing the right way would be good for me. My dear Aunt Chilly always took me for walks when I was growing up. She'd tell me to take a deep breath through my nose and imagine all the good, clean air I was taking in. She'd tell me to picture it cleaning everything from my veins and arteries to my bad feelings. Then Aunt Chilly would tell me to let that breath out through my mouth and imagine letting out all the bad germs and bad feelings. She'd ask me if I could see them leaving my mouth, and she was *so* convincing, I was sure that I could. I found that the breath-ing technique and visualization that Aunt Chilly had taught me as a child worked just as well when I was an adult. I used "in-with-the-good-and-out-with-the-bad" breathing as part of my daily routine. Later, I learned to meditate and indulge in those stress-relieving massages, manicures, and pedicures that I mentioned earlier.

Some of the best ways to recover from stress involve spending time with your loved ones. Even if you don't have common interests in the relationships that are important to you, it's never too late to start building them. Decide on an activity you'd like to learn together like golf or dance. Take an art class or a cooking class together. Become collectors together. Not only will you build another way to de-stress yourself, but you'll form stronger bonds and build beautiful memories with people you love.

You might ask, why do you have to learn these ways to recover from stress? Couldn't you just remove the stress at the source? Yes, I could and I did. But the thing about negative stress is that as soon as you alleviate it in one corner of your life, it will crop up somewhere else. Stressors, like choices and change, are going to keep on coming, so we have to learn how to manage them.

I have a very dear friend who learned to manage her stress by developing a chronic bronchial "illness." She told her family that her doctor had diagnosed this condition and had warned that if she didn't have at least one day a month of quiet bed rest to keep up her strength, the condition could become serious. She didn't have a bronchial condition, chronic or otherwise, but she desperately needed that time to recoup and de-stress from her daily living. For that one day a month, she lay in bed and read a book or watched movies. She didn't drive her kids to their friends' houses, she let the answering machine pick up phone messages . . . sometimes she didn't even shower or brush her teeth that day. She didn't do anything she didn't want to.

You may be a little shocked that she told her family such a whopper, or you might even think she was being selfish. Personally, I think she's one of the smartest women I know. Her family was very demanding of her time. She had to find a way to replenish herself—to be good to herself—so that she was mentally and emotionally strong enough to take care of her family the other twenty-nine or thirty days of every month. So she took some important R&R for one day. Everyone in her family managed just fine for that one day a month without her—they even catered to her. In return, she was able to cater to her family in a much more loving way the rest of the month. Just having her monthly day of R&R to look forward to made her daily stressors easier to manage.

Now maybe you can't fit in a full day to yourself every month—maybe the best you can do is to take a day every three months. At least you'll have that time to look forward to—and it's amazing how even thinking about the time off you're *going* to take can boost your positive thinking.

Quiet Time for You

For all your positive thoughts, strategies, and heart-to-heart talks with the mirror, you may still have a day that is really tough to get through. You know, the kind of day where the very best thing you can say about it is that it's over. At the end of that day, I really need some quiet time to myself. I tell my loved ones that I need some time alone. I sit in my most comfortable chair with a cup of my favorite tea. For a little while, I do my best not to think about the day. I just breathe in the good and breathe out the bad, relaxing in the comfort of being home. After a while, I review the day in my mind, just to see if there was some-thing I did that I could have done differently or better. And I do this only because I certainly don't want to repeat such a day if I don't have to. If I think of a better choice I could have made, I make a mental note to try that the next time. If I can't think of a thing I could have changed, then I say to myself, *Florine, just let it go. This, too, will pass and there is a tomorrow.*

When I can, I put on my most comfy pair of pajamas—even if it's only 6 P.M.—climb into my bed, and escape into a good book or an old movie. Those three things—comfy pajamas, my own bed, and a good book or movie—are my favorite de-stressors of all.

SELF-TEST: Are You De-Stressed or Distressed?

Rate the following questions from 1–5.

1 = Never or rarely

2 = A little of the time

3 = Some of the time

4 = A good part of the time

5 = Nearly all or all of the time

How often do you:

1. Feel like you're racing around from task to task, struggling to catch up? _____

2. Take time for yourself? _____

3. Feel overly frustrated or tense with your boss, the people you work with, family, or friends? _____

4. Lose your temper or cry? _____

5. Feel that you have a lot of responsibility but little authority or control? _____

6. End up being late for work or an appointment because you misplaced keys, files, or some other objects? _____

7. Find it difficult to concentrate because you have so much on your mind? _____

8. Start the day with a well-organized plan? _____

9. Put off making or keeping appointments with doctors or dentists? _____

10. Treat yourself to de-stressors—whether that's time with friends, a trip to a spa, a weekend getaway, and so on? _____

11. Beat yourself up over little mistakes? _____

12. Have panic attacks? _____

13. Find worry invading your thoughts even when you're trying to relax or go to sleep? _____

14. Obsess over little things? _____

15. Give yourself positive messages or experience positive stress? _____

Analysis

For numbers 1, 3, 4, 5, 6, 7, 9, 11, 12, 13, and 14, the lower your scores are, the fewer signs of negative stress you have. Scores of 1 or 2 are great, but several 3's probably mean that you've got too much negative stress in your life. Any score that rates a 4 or 5 is a specific area that deserves your attention.

For numbers 2, 8, 10, 15, the higher the score, the better. Answers of 4 or 5 are indicators that you are taking steps to keep your negative stress to a minimum or to de-stress. Low scores for these questions are further indicators of negative stress.

EXERCISE: In with the Good Air

Here's another great breathing exercise you can try. A yoga instructor once told me that most adults have forgotten how to breathe correctly. In fact, many of us breathe backward! This often happens because we're trying to hold in our stomachs or because of physical tension in our bodies.

If you look at a baby or an animal breathing, you'll see that when they breathe in, their stomachs expand out. When they let out a breath, their stomachs come back down. This way of breathing is not only the way nature intended, but yoga practitioners believe that proper breathing promotes health and reduces tension.

You can get back in the habit of proper breathing. Simply rest your hand on your stomach or upper abdomen and take a breath in through your nose. You should feel your stomach expand against your hand. When you breathe out, you should feel your stomach come back down.

Then practice, practice, practice!

Some Great Resources

The Highly Sensitive Person by Elaine Aron

How to Keep People from Pushing Your Buttons by Albert Ellis

Minimize Stress, Maximize Success: Effective Strategies for Realizing Your Goals by Clare Harris

Move Your Stuff, Change Your Life: How to Use Feng Shui to Get Love, Money, Respect and Happiness by Karen Rauch Carter

Organizing from the Inside Out by Julie Morgenstern

Relax—You May Only Have a Few Minutes Left: Using the Power of Humor to Overcome Stress in Your Life and Work by Loretta Laroche

10

When Love Hurts

*The ultimate test of a relationship is to
disagree but to hold hands.*
—Alexandra Penney

*Love is a moment and a lifetime. Love is working together,
laughing together, growing together. Love is wanting to shout
from the rooftops the successes, little and big, of one another.
Love is wanting to wipe away the tears when failures comes.
Love is laughter, especially in the middle of a quarrel.*
—Liz Carpenter

*Love doesn't make the world go round.
Love is what makes the ride worthwhile.*
—Franklin P. Jones

So far, I've talked a lot about all the wonderful things
that love can do for us. Love can help us get more joy out

of our days, it can help us take the distress out of stress, and when we love ourselves, it can even help us to be as forgiving of ourselves as we are of others. There is a reason that Shakespeare spent all that time writing sonnets, that so many love songs go to the top of the charts, and that self-help books on how to get more love can become best sellers. Love is great stuff. But love, like anything that is worth having, comes at a price.

Anytime we love, we make ourselves vulnerable. That's the price we have to be willing to pay. If a friend or family member says something that hurts our feelings, it hurts so much more *because* we love them. We care what they think and how they feel about us. When we become parents, the 2 A.M. feedings and mountains of diapers are nothing compared to the fear and pain we feel when our babies are crying inconsolably and we don't know why. Underneath it all, we think, *What if something is wrong with my child that can't be fixed? What will I do?* And when someone we love passes away, it feels as if a piece of us goes with them. These are all times when love hurts.

The painful side of love is one of the biggest curveballs that life can throw us. While we can't prevent that pain, we can learn how to manage it . . . and sometimes even how to make our lives stronger and richer for it.

Stopping the Pain

The question you need to ask yourself when love hurts is, *What can I do to stop the pain?* Sometimes we have that power and sometimes we don't have that power. If there is friction between a family member and you, it's easier to stop the pain when you understand who created the friction to begin with—the family member, you, or both of you.

It's possible to find yourself on the receiving end of anger when you haven't done a thing to deserve it. You're trying to referee an argument between your kids and suddenly they both turn on you. Your husband has had a bad day at work and when he walks in the door, you get the brunt of his anger. In both situations, you're just standing there taking it in while trying not to become angry and abusive yourself, because you know it will just make matters worse. It helps tremendously if you can keep in mind that this isn't about you. They're just taking it out on you because they know that you're a safe place to vent their frustrations. They know you'll love them anyway. This *sounds* simple . . . I know it's not. No matter how much you love someone, no matter how much you realize that her tirade isn't about you, it *hurts* when the people we love lash out at us.

This is when it's time to head for the mirror—quick. Take a deep breath and say, *This is not about you. You were just in the wrong place at the wrong time. It's obvious that they're having a bad time—just let them vent. They don't usually do this— they must be very upset. Let it go.* I know that when I use the mirror to talk myself down, it really does help me put the situation into perspective. Getting that perspective is usually enough to keep me from bringing more anger to an already difficult situation.

Of course, it's a very different matter if they *do* usually take out their anger and frustration on me. If lashing out at me has become a habit, not only can I stop the pain, I feel that I have a responsibility to myself to stop the pain. If I find myself becoming someone's personal whipping post, then I know I have to take action. I'll bring it to the person's attention and try my very best to talk it out and work it out. But if after that, the person's still saying hurtful things or doing things that make me uncomfortable, I stop putting myself in that situation. That may mean spending less time or even no time with that person.

If you're in a relationship where you are uncomfortable much or most of the time, there is no way to get joy out of each day. In fact, being in an uncomfortable relationship for any length of time can start to affect the quality of your other relationships, and who can afford to let that happen? Who would *want* to let that happen?

Find the Source of the Pain

It's especially important to find out why there is friction between someone you love and you. I work with a woman named Mary Beth who, until recently, was a stay-at-home mom. Her best friend, Carolyn, and she became inseparable from the moment they first met in high school. Fifteen years later, they still lived in the same neighborhood, shared many of the same friends, and even took turns watching each other's kids to build in some relaxation time for themselves.

When Mary Beth's youngest daughter entered first grade last year, she decided to go back to work and landed a terrific job in marketing. Suddenly, Mary Beth's days went from peanut butter sandwiches and Winnie the Pooh to corporate events and power lunches. Her relationship with Carolyn also went right down the tubes, and at first, Mary Beth had no idea why. It's hard to ask, "Why are you so mad at me?" but to her credit, Mary Beth did just that. Carolyn completely denied being angry and even implied that Mary Beth was just looking for attention. But Carolyn continued to behave negatively. When Mary Beth asked her what she'd done that day, she got short, terse responses like, "Nothing that *you'd* find very interesting." Then, when Mary Beth tried to make conversation by talking about her own day, Carolyn would just cut her off. Mary Beth got the feeling that Carolyn had even begun avoiding her. Finally, Mary Beth decided that enough was enough—it was time to deal with the tension between them head-on. Mary Beth said, "Don't tell me you're not mad—it's obvious that you are. You're my best friend and I love you. I'm not letting what we have fall apart because you don't want to talk about it. I'm not leaving until we have this out." Carolyn promptly burst into tears. She'd been having a lot of negative emotions about Mary Beth's new job. Part of it was a feeling that she was being abandoned because Mary Beth was no longer giving her the weekday breaks she'd become used to having. Plus, when Mary Beth went back to work, Carolyn felt guilty for wanting to still be a stay-at-home mom and intimidated by what she saw as Mary Beth's new status.

When Mary Beth understood the reasons for Carolyn's anger, she was able to talk calmly with Carolyn to work things out. Carolyn's feelings weren't really about anything that Mary Beth had done; they were about Carolyn's own needs, feelings, and insecurities. Carolyn was having bad feelings about her own life and taking those feelings out on Mary Beth—someone she admired and trusted to still love her in spite of the way she was behaving. Mary Beth told Carolyn that she would never knowingly do anything to hurt her. Mary Beth reminded her that just because going back to work was right for her, it didn't mean it was right for Carolyn. Mary Beth even offered to have Carolyn's kids over to her house one evening each week so that Carolyn could have some relaxation time. She told her that going to the office five days a week was not nearly as tough as being a stay-at-home mom 24/7. Yes, it was a painful experience for them both, but Mary Beth had the perseverance, patience, and caring to help her friend work through her feelings. I'm happy to report that today Mary Beth and Carolyn are closer than ever.

When You Need to Stop Yourself from Hurting Others

Sometimes we're not on the receiving end of anger. Sometimes *we're* the ones causing the pain when we lash out at our loved ones. We lose our temper, become impatient, or make critical remarks because we have had a bad day, have too much to get done, aren't feeling well, or just plain aren't thinking. If you find yourself losing control—saying things to your loved ones that you know you shouldn't say—you might try the motivational author Og Mandino's strategy: "Treat everyone as if they were going to be dead by midnight. Your life will never be the same again." The more respect you can have for others and yourself, the more you'll be able to stop yourself from hurting the ones you love.

Sometimes we hurt our loved ones without even being aware of it. Just because we may have managed to hold back saying angry words doesn't mean we haven't given a loved one an angry message. We can send out negative signals that deliver our feelings just as clearly as if we'd spoken harsh words. Anger can come across in the tone of our voices, in the way we use our hands when we speak, or when we fold our arms tightly and defensively across our chests. We need to figure out what's really bothering us and deal with those problems head-on instead of taking out all those bad feelings on the people who matter to us the most.

If you're going to ask a loved one what you've done to offend or upset him, be prepared to hear the answer. Criticism can be hard to take. Don't automatically defend yourself, which is usually our very first impulse. Tell him that you need to think about what he said, and give yourself some time to think it over. If you really don't believe that what he said is true, sit down and try to talk it out to reach an understanding. If the criticism is true, apologize with all your heart, make amends, and try your best not to repeat the offense. It is hoped that in time you'll be able to repair or, if necessary, even rebuild your relationship. If you honestly don't know whether the criticism is true, take your own small survey. Ask people you trust to be honest about whether you've done something wrong or behaved badly. Again, be prepared to hear the answer. There is a colorful old saying: "If one person calls me an ass, I can ignore him; if ten people call me an ass, I'd better buy myself a saddle." None of us is perfect. Admit when you're wrong, work to overcome your imperfections, and ask your loved ones to forgive and forget your mistakes.

Nip Pain in the Bud

Ultimately, we've got to do everything we can to stop the pain of harboring anger between our loved ones and ourselves. There is a story about a church minister who had two brothers in his congregation. He always saw the brothers sitting on opposite sides of the church and learned from a parishioner that the brothers hadn't spoken to each other in twenty-five years. He just couldn't understand the rift—they were both such nice people. One Christmas, the minister made a vow to get the brothers together. He called one to his office and said, "Look, it's Christmas. In the spirit of the season, isn't it time for you both to make amends? I'd really like to help bring you two together. Now tell me what went wrong between you and your brother?" The man said, "I don't know, but it must have been really terrible because we haven't spoken in twenty-five years." Isn't that sad? Two such nice men wasted twenty-five years of togetherness, and they couldn't even remember why.

Nip disagreements in the bud. Forgive and forget an offense that was done to you. Ask to be forgiven for offending someone else. Talk it out. Argue it out if necessary . . . but don't give up on someone you love. If you've given it your all, and he still doesn't want to reconcile, be nice to him. Leave the door open between you so he knows that he can walk back through it in the future. Then make peace with yourself and live your life.

When You See Others Hurting Themselves

We've talked about positive ways in which we can respond when we've been hurt and when we've been hurtful. But there is another kind of hurt. That is the pain we feel when we watch our loved ones make choices that will hurt them.

When my children were growing up, I was the chief operating officer of our family. I was responsible for its day-to-day operations. Like most mothers, I managed nearly everything in my kids' lives—food, clothing, bedtimes, medical care. I had the job of making decisions for them to protect their well-being. I may not have always made the right choices, but whatever choice I made was done with love.

Eventually, my children grew up and it was time for me to be promoted to chairman of the board. I no longer had to make decisions for them—they became the chief operating officers of their own lives (and their children's lives, too!). The upside is that now I can focus on making my own life the best it can be. I don't have to worry that I'll make a bad decision for them or tell them that there is something they can't do or have. My days of having to say no are over. The downside is that sometimes I have to watch my children make decisions that my experience tells me will probably make them unhappy in the end. I make it a point not to give my opinion unless they ask for it. When they do ask, I make sure to preface my opinion with the fact that it's just that—my opinion. I'm not in any way trying to tell them what to do because it's *completely* their decision. The best I can do is respectfully caution them about the course of action they're planning. I make a suggestion to give them something to think about and tell them that I'm proud of them and that I know they'll make the right decision for themselves. Sometimes they take my suggestions and sometimes they don't. If they don't take my suggestion and all ends well, I'm so happy to have been proven wrong. If their choice doesn't work out the way they hoped, I'm there for them.

Being there for my children means doing everything I can to make them feel better or to make things easier for them. I start by *not* saying *I told you so*. That is one sentence that should be banned from your vocabulary, too, because saying it has never helped anyone. Be there for your loved ones to listen, offer them whatever support you can, and tell them you love them. You have the power to make it easier for them to cope with the consequences of their choices.

That scenario holds true not only for parents talking to their adult children but for friends talking to friends, adult children talking to parents, coworkers talking to coworkers, siblings talking to siblings—*any* loved ones you see heading for disaster. You can offer suggestions but you can't *force* them to follow them. After that, all you can do is watch—and if your worst fears are realized, it can be so painful. It's another time that love really hurts . . . and one time that you may be powerless to prevent their pain.

When Loved Ones Get Sick or Hurt

The other kind of pain that we have limited power to stop is when someone we love gets sick or hurt. That's a pain I know all too well. Last year, my husband, Bill—the love of my life—was diagnosed with amyotrophic lateral sclerosis (ALS), more commonly known as Lou Gehrig's disease. ALS is a disease that causes progressive nerve and muscle weakness, and, as of this writing, there is no cure.

We were shocked when Bill got this terrible diagnosis. He was an energetic, fun-loving man who'd always taken care of his health. He ate right, exercised daily, and saw his doctor regularly. Then suddenly, his whole life was turned upside down. He couldn't do the things he enjoyed most, like playing tennis or golfing. His legs became weak and he tired easily. Just a few months before, everything had seemed fine. Then suddenly, we were living day by day, hour by hour, and minute by minute, coping with this disease. It was devastating for him to experience and devastating for me to watch. It's at times like this that love hurts the most.

But Bill decided to handle what life had thrust upon him with all the dignity and grace that he possibly could. I've made the same commitment. We were partners in life and in love, and we lived each day in the hope that we'd have many more to live together.

We did not take this diagnosis lying down. Bill didn't get his diagnosis and simply ask the doctor, "Now what do I do?" He got a second and even a third opinion. He asked for extensive tests to give him as much information as he could get about his condition and possible treatment options. Bill and I were constantly on the phone, on the Internet, or at the library to learn more about ALS, to seek out doctors who specialize in treating the disease, and to find new treatments and clinical trials. We recruited all our family and friends to join us in these searches. We networked with other families who were battling the disease to learn from their experience and to share what we'd learned. We hosted benefits to raise money for research. We lived in the hope that a cure for ALS would be found in our lifetimes.

But that was not to be. Bill passed away in March from complications of the disease. You may wonder how I feel about all the time and effort that Bill and I spent looking for a cure. After all, we didn't find a cure in time to save him. The answer is that given the same set of circumstances, I'd spend our time together in exactly the same way.

We took control of what we could, accepted what we couldn't control, and lived together in love each and every day Bill was alive. And who knows? Maybe someday there will be a cure—maybe someday, someone with ALS will return to a full, healthy life with his loved ones because of the efforts of people like Bill and myself. As a man who dedicated his life to healing others, that would mean the world to Bill.

One thing I learned from this experience is that there is more to truly great doctors than their knowledge of medicine. Truly great doctors—like Bill—combine the expertise of science with the art of listening to their patients and empathizing with their feelings. We don't need medical degrees to practice that same art at home. We can combine giving our loved ones the physical care they need with just *listening* to them and being there for them.

Just Be There

Bill showed me what a difference just being there for someone can make—for the person and for us. One day Bill had to go to the hospital because of a fall. While he was in the emergency room, he learned that a friend of his was also there. His friend had been suffering from multiple sclerosis but was in the emergency room because he had also just suffered a heart attack. Instead of dwelling on his own problems, Bill went to console his friend, listening to his concerns and just being there for him. It was good medicine for them both.

Some mornings we'd wake up feeling a little down. He'd ask me how I was feeling and I'd ask him how he was feeling, and we'd admit to each other that it was a little tough to start the day feeling positive. So we'd march into the mirror together and I'd say, "Good morning, Bill! It's a beautiful day!" And

he'd say, "Good morning, Florine! It's going to be a great day!"
By then, we'd usually be smiling—maybe even laughing.

If you or someone you love is facing a life-threatening illness, talking to the mirror can help you cope with your emotions. Some days the talk I mentioned above may be enough to lift your spirits, and when it is, that's great. When that talk isn't enough, that's okay, too. Don't dismiss your feelings or try to hide them inside. Be honest with yourself. Say it out loud and deal with it. *I'm depressed. Now what am I going to do about it? I'm not going to waste a whole day feeling like this.* Cry and get it out. Jump up and down. Make funny faces at yourself in the mirror. The point is to relieve the tension and anxiety that builds up in all of us at times like these.

It's often said that something good can come out of even the worst times. In our case we found that after the diagnosis, we were more grateful for every single moment of every single day that we had together. We were always grateful for everything we had; we always tried to live every day to the fullest . . . but after the diagnosis, even more so. We held hands more. We spent more time watching sunrises and sunsets. Everything seemed exaggerated. Every day that we were together the sun seemed to shine a little brighter, the grass was greener, raindrops sounded more beautiful, and flowers smelled sweeter.

We never had one heated discussion after Bill's diagnosis. To be honest, they just seemed frivolous. We didn't want to waste any time being unhappy. There just wasn't anything that was worth arguing about. So why was anything worth arguing over before the diagnosis?

If I could take any moral out of the story, it would be this: don't wait for a catastrophic diagnosis to become more grateful for everyone and everything around you.

Of course you can't go through every moment of every day thinking about how wonderful life is. Stressful moments and events will get in the way. But at least once each day, stop and smell the roses of your life. Be grateful for who you are and what you have. Even as I mourn losing Bill, I am so grateful for every moment I had with him.

Sometimes love hurts, but love can also heal our hearts and souls, and it can heal the hearts and souls of the people who matter most to us. Love is what life is all about.

EXERCISE: Build a Bridge, Mend a Fence,
Make a Connection

To be honest, this is less of an exercise and more of an invitation. Think about the people you love. Not just the people that you get to love every day but all the people you've loved in your life. Odds are there is at least one whom you've lost touch with. Maybe she offended you, maybe you offended her, or maybe you simply lost touch because life got hectic. Today is the day to pick up the phone and call her.

If you don't know what to say, start with hello, and let her know you've been thinking of her. If you owe her an apology, make one. If she owes you an apology, don't ask for one. Instead, imagine that she is going to be dead by midnight. Does the apology still seem so important? If it does, maybe you need to talk about it. But remember, you called her. It's up to you to make the first step toward reconciliation. Worry less about who was right and who was wrong, and focus more about what it's going to take to mend your relationship.

If she rejects your best attempt to reconnect, it's time to make peace with the situation, knowing that you tried to set things right. Wish her well and be kind when you say good-bye. Leave a door open in your heart. Someday you just might pick up the phone to find she's on the other end.

If it's not a matter of a disagreement but you've just lost

touch, make time to catch up. Set a time to talk on the phone or meet in person, and make sure you make keeping the appointment a priority.

If you manage to reconnect with that person, commit to nurturing the relationship. If she was important enough to contact, she's important enough to keep. Take joy in this new beginning.

Some Great Resources

The Anger Control Workbook by Peter Rogers

The Anger Habit Workbook: Proven Principles to Calm the Stormy Mind by Carl D. Semmelroth

Handbook for Mortals: Guidance for People Facing Serious Illness by Joanne Lynn

Love: What Life Is All About by Leo F. Buscaglia

Loving Your Partner Without Losing Your Self by Martha Baldwin Beveridge

Keeping the Love You Find by Harville Hendrix

PART III

MAKING FRIENDS WITH YOUR FUTURE

*One's self-image is very important because if that's in good
shape, then you can do practically anything.*
—SIR JOHN GIELGUD

*We either make ourselves miserable or make
ourselves strong. The amount of work is the same.*
—CARLOS CASTANEDA

*Show me someone who doesn't dream about
the future and I'll show you someone who
doesn't know where she is going.*
—ANONYMOUS

*I've always been in the right place at the right time.
Of course I steered myself there.*
—BOB HOPE

THE HUMORIST AND SPEECHWRITER Robert Orben once said, "We have enough people who tell it like it is . . . we need more people to tell it like it can be." That's why I wrote this book—and why I wrote this part in particular. I want to be your advocate for the future—to help you make your future the very best that it can be.

If you're not satisfied with what you've done in your past, looking toward the future can be a little bit scary. To start with, you may feel insecure about just how much better you can make your future. And if you're in your thirties, forties, or older, unwanted thoughts may start creeping in about how many years you have left. *Have I already reached the halfway mark?* The truth is that we do only get so many years on this earth, none of us—no matter what our age—knows exactly how many years we've got left, and we can't get back the years we've already spent. What we *can* do is change how we spend our time from now on.

Every morning you wake up is a new opportunity for change. By planning correctly, taking action on that plan, and keeping a positive attitude, you can grab hold of that opportunity to make your future so much better than yesterday or today.

As part of that planning, I'm going to ask you to take a look at all the areas of your life that are working for you *and* the areas that may be holding you back. The problem is that "looking" and "seeing" are two different things. You may have certain flaws that you find too painful to face; or you could be turning a few molehill flaws into mountainous defects. Before you can begin to plan for a better future, you'll need to put your flaws and your assets—and we all have both—into perspective. How can you know what you need to change until you see yourself as you truly are?

Before you can carry out any plan for the future, it's a good idea to unload emotional baggage that you picked up in the past—baggage that may still be weighing you down today. It's time to lighten that load before starting on your journey to a better tomorrow.

Whatever plan you decide on can be made or broken by your attitude toward the future, especially when it comes to aging. Slowing down, gaining weight, and settling for the same old status quo are all negative signs of aging—and I've seen thirty-year-olds who display all those signs and ninety-year-olds who don't. You have no control over getting older, but you do have control over what getting older means. If you're getting old before your time, it's time to stop counting the breaths you take and, as the saying goes, start counting the times that life takes your breath away.

Your attitude about the past can affect your plans for the future, too. They may say that living well is the best revenge, but the truth is that in a well-lived life, there is no room for looking backward in bitterness. You'll move your plans that much further ahead when you face the future with a happy and hopeful heart, looking ahead toward all you can accomplish and the rewards you'll enjoy for journeys made, changes navigated, and obstacles overcome.

Whatever plans you make, however you decide to change the course of your life from here, one thing is certain: now is the time to make friends with your future.

11

MIRROR, MIRROR ON THE WALL, AM I SEEING ME AT ALL?

Self-knowledge is the beginning of self-improvement.
—SPANISH PROVERB

Knowing others is wisdom.
Knowing yourself is enlightenment.
—LAO TZU

Be yourself. No one can ever tell you
you're doing it wrong.
—JAMES LEO HERLIHY

We must be trying to learn who we really are rather
than trying to tell ourselves who we should be.
—JOHN POWELL

IN PART I, I ASKED YOU to look in the mirror and describe to me the person who you saw. On the surface, that may have sounded like a simple enough task, but in practice, facing our-selves in the mirror can be quite a challenge. After all, *looking* in the mirror is one thing, but really *seeing* ourselves is much more difficult.

It has often been said that each of us is really three people—the person we see ourselves to be, the person others see us to be, and who we really are. Let's talk about getting a clearer vision of the person each of us sees in the mirror. It's time to get rid of all the stuff that gets in the way of seeing ourselves as we truly are. Only when we do this can we truly know what we want and need for the future.

So what can get in the way of seeing ourselves clearly when we look in the mirror?

Weight Issues

Sometimes our flaws are just too painful to face. When I was fifty pounds overweight, I knew that I had a weight problem, but most of the time I didn't *see* myself as being as overweight as I was. I tried to distract myself by trying to improve my looks from the neck up so that I wouldn't have to deal with the problem I was having from the neck down. I made it a point *not* to look in full-length mirrors—I didn't even keep them in my room. I put all my efforts into finding the best color to dye my hair and wearing my hair in styles that would make my face look thinner (at least I convinced myself that it looked thinner). I bought the most flattering eye makeup I could find and the prettiest blushes and lipsticks. I wore earrings that drew atten-tion up to my face. Not only did *I* spend all my time looking at everything above the neck, I guess I hoped that's where others would focus their attention, too.

The truth is that we can't fool others about how much we weigh. Most of the time, we can tell whether someone is overweight, underweight, or the right weight with just one look. Wearing dark colors, control-top pantyhose, and vertical stripes might help a little bit, but it's not going to completely hide our being twenty, thirty, fifty pounds or more overweight from anyone—except maybe from ourselves.

If you've been using tricks like these to hide from your weight problem, it's time to take a good, hard, honest look at yourself. Lock the door to your room, undress, go to a full-length mirror and take a look at yourself as you really are. If you don't like what you see, it's time to face the problem and make a commitment to lose the weight and get healthier. You'll be amazed at how much extra time and energy you will have to enjoy your life when you're not spending so much time and energy on trying to hide your weight problem.

As important as it is to face your flaws, it is equally important to see the real you once you've fixed the problem. It's not good to be too easy on yourself—but it can be just as bad when you're too hard on yourself. We shouldn't keep beating ourselves up for things that we can't change.

I've been at my goal weight for more than twenty-five years, but trying on bathing suits is still the quickest way to ruin my day. When I was in my thirties, I had to have a hysterectomy, and the surgery left me with a little tummy that even with daily exercise, I was never able to get rid of. Beyond that, the women in my family tend to be pear-shaped—we carry all our weight below the waist. So even at a healthy weight, I'm curvier in the hip area than I'd like to be. Putting on a bathing suit in front of a three-sided mirror calls my attention to all the flaws that I still have.

It's especially easy for me to blow my flaws out of proportion when I'm looking at a fashion magazine. I have to remind myself that 99 percent of the women in the world don't look like supermodels. Did you know that besides being beautiful, most supermodels are over five nine, small-boned, and about twenty pounds underweight? How many women could meet all those standards . . . even if they wanted to?

Remarkable Woman Anthea Paul, author and founder of *Girlosophy*, spent years in the high-fashion industry. She says that even the supermodels themselves aren't as perfect as they seem. "People forget that the advertisements they see in fashion magazines aren't photos as much as they are visual works of art," says Anthea. "There is a whole team that creates the illusions within that picture. Two weeks can be spent just getting the setting to look right. When the model comes in for the shoot, a team of stylists works on her hair, nails, and makeup to get the exact look the shot calls for. Techs can spend hours making sure that the lighting on the model is flattering from all directions. Even then, the photo itself is altered to remove the model's every blemish, make her skin appear smoother, enhance her breasts, whiten her eyes, and almost anything else you can think of before the shot is considered ready to print. Not even supermodels look like the supermodels you see in magazines."

If I allow myself to turn my molehill flaws into mountainous defects, I'm clouding the picture of the real me just as much as I did when I refused to see my weight problem. So when I look at my body in the mirror, I make sure that I look at the good of me as much as I look at the things about me that I'd like to change—but can't. So I have a little tummy and curvy hips—I also have a small waist, nice legs, slender ankles, and pretty eyes.

Each of us has things that we like about the way we look—and some things we don't. Sure, we should change what we can for the better, but we need to stop beating ourselves up about what we *can't* change and look into the mirror with a real appreciation for all the things we have going for us. We're so quick to talk about what's wrong with our bodies, but many of us are embarrassed to say what's right with our bodies. It's not vain to acknowledge the things that we love about ourselves— it creates the balance we need to see ourselves as we truly are.

Some people look into the mirror and never see themselves as being thin enough, or they buy into the idea that you can never be too thin, but you know that's just not true. Too much of anything can be bad for you, whether it's too much weight or too much weight loss. That's why Weight Watchers provides its members with weight ranges that include the healthy maximum and *minimum* weight for your height. If you're not a Weight Watchers member, your doctor can tell you what your weight range should be. If your doctor's recommendation matches your idea of what you should weigh, then you'll know you're seeing 20/20.

Dealing with Other Issues

If your problem is related to something other than weight, you can talk to professionals in those areas, too. If you've got debt, see a debt counselor; if you think you've chosen the wrong major in school, see a guidance counselor; if you've got conflict in your marriage, see a marriage counselor. These are non-biased individuals who can help you work through your issues to find a solution that is right for you.

Loved ones can also provide helpful advice as we try to solve the problems we've seen within ourselves *and* draw our attention the problems we've yet to see. I had a nervous habit of clearing my throat when I was giving a speech. My father-in-law was kind enough to call that habit to my attention. He said, "Florine, you have a lot of good things to say but when you clear your throat, it's very distracting." As it turned out, he also had a suggestion to help me fix the problem. As an opera singer, he had learned that when you feel the need to clear your throat, raising the pitch of your voice one step will often make the sensation go away. I tried it and found that my father-in-law was right—it really worked! When loved ones offer us constructive criticism, we owe it to them *and* to ourselves to hear them out.

Still, sometimes it's important to take advice with a grain of salt. Remember, each of us is really three people: the person we see, the person others see, and the person we truly are. The writer Anaïs Nin said, "We don't always see things as they are; we see them as *we* are." That can be a problem. It's sometimes tough to separate the real you from the you that others perceive. Just because they see us in a certain way—*their* way—doesn't make it true.

Take birth order for example. It is common to treat the youngest child in the family as "the baby" long after childhood is over. Parents and even siblings sometimes treat the youngest as needing to be sheltered or looked after. That's fine when they're three but not very healthy when they're thirty. That kind of overprotectiveness generally has less to do with how capable the youngest is and more to do with the need for parents to hold on to parenting.

It is also not unusual for a family to treat the oldest child as somehow being more capable and more responsible than the younger children in the family. I can tell you that as the oldest, I was always given the message that I should be able to handle any situation that came along. Like most things, there was an upside and a downside to that message. The upside was that I was lucky to have parents, grandparents, aunts, and uncles who always cheered me on, telling me that I could accomplish anything I wanted. The downside is that when something really bad happens—something that is more than I can handle alone—I tend to try to tough out the situation too long before asking for help. No one has *ever* told me that I shouldn't ask for help, and I've gotten help anytime I asked for it. But my birth order has had an impact on the way others see me and, ultimately, the way I see myself.

All that being said, it's never too late to change those perceptions. The middle child usually gets the worst deal when it comes to birth order. She's called the lost child, the troubled child, the child most likely to be messed up—not flattering descriptions, to say the least. A friend of mine who happens to be a middle child has come up with her own definition of what it means to be a middle child. She refers to herself as "the child who brings balance." What a wonderful message to give herself and those around her. She had the courage to redefine herself, and you can do the same. You do not have to let others' perceptions of you become your reality.

Sometimes that's easier said than done. People's mental habits—the way that they've come to think about people and things—are just as difficult to change as physical habits. If your father has always seen you as the baby of the family, don't expect his perception of you to change with one conversation. Give those around you at least the same four months of reinforcing your new image before you can expect to see their vision of you change. You just have to keep reminding them that although you may be the youngest, you are an adult.

In the meantime, don't be surprised if you get some resistance from your loved ones when you behave in ways that go against their vision of who you are and what's best for you.

Ann's Story

I know a woman named Ann who was the youngest in her family. By the time she graduated from high school, her sister and two brothers had already left home. She had saved some money for college and won some scholarships, but she was going to have to take out loans to afford room and board on campus. She was relieved when her parents offered to let her continue to live at home while going to the local college. After college, Ann found an entry-level position at an accounting firm. Her parents suggested that she continue to live at home and put some money in savings before getting her own place. Although Ann really wanted her own apartment by this time, she had to admit that her parents' suggestion made good financial sense. Ann tried to pay rent and help with the utilities, but her parents wouldn't take the money. When she tried to talk it over with her father, his only answer was, "You don't have to worry—we'll take care of you." Ann was very grateful for her parents' love and support, but after a while, she began to feel uncomfortable still living at home. Whenever she tried to talk about this, her father would cut her off, telling her that she wasn't ready to live on her own.

At age twenty-six, Ann decided that it was now time to move into her own home. She had saved so much money over the last four years that she was able to start shopping for a house instead of renting an apartment. She still hadn't worked up the nerve to tell her parents. One day, the real estate agent called to tell Ann about a new house on the market, and her father took the message.

Her father was furious. At first Ann thought he was just angry because she hadn't told him about what she was doing, but soon she realized that he was angry that she was leaving home. Ann told me, "That's when Dad said some pretty mean things to me. He told me that I couldn't make it on my own and that I'd end up having a house to unload when I found out I couldn't handle it. I was crushed." Ann also started to have self-doubts. Could she afford this house? Could she afford to live on her own? She had always trusted her father's advice, and if he didn't think she could handle it, maybe she couldn't. Ann finally went to her mirror one day and started talking to herself about the situation.

Ann said, "I started reminding myself about my accomplishments. I'd graduated from college with honors, landed a job as soon as I'd graduated, and gotten very good performance reviews at work. Sure, I had the advantage of living at home, but I could have squandered my money . . . and I didn't. I'd been responsible enough to save more than half of what I'd earned. Then I tried to think of reasons why I wouldn't be able to make it on my own . . . and I couldn't come up with one. That's when I realized this wasn't about *me*—it was about the way that Dad still *sees* me."

Ann tried to talk to her father. She tried to help him understand that although she'd always be *his* baby, she wasn't a baby anymore. Unfortunately, she didn't get very far at the time—her father wasn't speaking to her when she moved out.

Ann moved, and as soon as she got settled in, she invited her parents to dinner in her new home. Her mother came—but her father didn't. Her mother simply said, "Give him time, dear." The next time Ann invited her parents to dinner, she was surprised when her dad came. "He looked for everything he could find wrong with the house, but at least he came!" Ann laughed.

It took awhile, but eventually her father came to realize that he wasn't losing Ann. She maintained her independence but continued spending time with her family. Ann told me that her proudest moment came at Thanksgiving when she heard her father bragging to her uncle about the great deal she'd gotten on her house and how good she was with money.

Weigh the Pros and Cons

Be honest with yourself as you weigh all the pros and cons before making your decision. If your loved ones disagree with a course of action you're considering, talk to the mirror about whether there is merit to what your loved ones are telling you. Ask yourself, "Am I letting my pride get in the way of listening to what they say? Is my ego holding me back from listening to the truth?" If they are right, find the courage to say to them, "I've thought about what you've said and you were right. I was wrong. I'm going to do what you recommend." It's okay to admit you were wrong—in fact, it's more than okay. There is a wise old adage that says, "To admit you were wrong is to declare that you are wiser now than before."

On the other hand, if you know in your heart that what you're doing is right for you, like Ann, you have to stick to your guns. When it comes down to it, this is *your* life, and, as far as anybody knows, it's the only life you're going to have. Ultimately, you've got to decide what's right for you and continue on your life's path as you think best.

After the Clear View Mirror

I think it's important that we take a little time to talk about what happens *after* you've started seeing yourself more clearly. What do you do when you've taken that honest look in the mirror and seen those things that you need to change? To use George Bernard Shaw's words, "Life isn't about finding yourself—it's about *creating* yourself." Sometimes we need to start over, *re*-creating ourselves so that we can live a more satisfying future.

Maybe you're a junior in college but you've realized that the major you chose was a mistake; maybe you lost a lot of weight but gained it all back—plus ten pounds; maybe you decided to be a stay-at-home mom but now your kids are grown and you realize you have nothing to do at home; or maybe that 70/30 balance in your marriage has shifted to 30/70 and you've realized that there is no shifting it back.

Starting over is always scary, but for me, divorce was the scariest of them all. I'd been "Sadie, Sadie, married lady" for most of my life, so facing life on my own seemed like a completely foreign idea. During the day, I worried about the big questions like where I was going to live, how I was going to support myself, and what the divorce would mean to my children. At night when I couldn't sleep, even little questions that may seem silly in comparison to the big questions, really got to me. *Who will I go to the movies with? What if someone invites me to a wedding—will anyone dance with me? Everyone I know invites people to parties as couples—will I still get invitations? If I do and I have to go alone, will I feel like a third wheel?* Boy, did I talk to the mirror a lot in those days.

It was one of those talks that changed my perspective and helped me to move forward with my life. I asked the mirror, *How can I make the best of starting over?* The first thing I did—and I think this is good for anyone who is starting over in any way—was admit to myself that I was scared. That was hard for me. I always wanted to believe that I could cope with whatever happens and that I could do it all by myself.

But you know what? No one should have to face something as scary as starting over alone. Talk to your family, friends, clergy, a counselor—talk to your mirror. Be honest about the fact that you're afraid. Talking it out helps to keep all those fears that are floating around in your head from getting the best of you.

I have a dear cousin who is battling cancer. In a way, she had to start over after getting her diagnosis. She had to start over as a person fighting to overcome a life-threatening illness. She's had surgery and is now going through chemotherapy. When I called her the other day, I asked if she was up to talking and she said, "Oh, yes—please keep calling. I don't know if I could do this without everyone that I have on my side."

Don't try to be a hero by going it alone. I guess some people can go it alone, but why would you want to? Why go it alone when others can make things easier?

The other thing I did for myself when I was starting over was to talk myself into becoming an even more enthusiastic person. I've always been enthusiastic—I think it helps your life at work and at home. I made a conscious decision not to view my divorce as an ending but as a new beginning. Starting over can be a real adventure . . . it all depends on how you decide to look at it.

Pam, a friend of mine who was a very shy, quiet person, found that she had to relocate with her husband because he was being transferred to an office in another city. At the time, she was six months pregnant with their first child and scared to death by the idea of this new start. All she could think about were the uncertainties. Questions whirled around in her mind: *Where will we live? Will I be able to find a good obstetrician? How far is the nearest hospital and will it be a good hospital? I won't know anyone there—will I be able to make friends? Will I be able to find my way around?* As I said, Pam was shy to begin with—but being pregnant made her feel especially vulnerable about starting over hundreds of miles from her family and friends.

When they arrived in their new city, Pam saw that her husband had found them a terrific house in a tree-lined neighborhood. For the first time, she started to see things a little more positively. She worked up her courage to knock on her neighbor's door to introduce herself, and she received a warm welcome. Before she could walk over to see the neighbor on the other side of her house, the neighbor met her halfway with a cake she'd baked. Her neighbors set up a tea so that Pam could meet the other women in the neighborhood. They talked about the best doctors in the area, where to shop for groceries, and the fact that there was a beautiful baby boutique in town.

Before she knew it, Pam had gotten into the swing of getting her new home in order, spending time with her new friends, and preparing to welcome her baby into the world. It turned out to be a wonderful new start.

Your New Start

When you find yourself worrying about the new start you're making, talk to the mirror. Remind yourself that most of the things we worry about never happen.

Instead, get enthusiastic about every opportunity to start over. See the new beginning for what it truly is: a new chance to build the life you want to live. The author Henry Chester said that "enthusiasm is the strongest asset in the world. It beats money and power and influence." Enthusiasm has helped me in literally every aspect of my life, from raising my children to starting a business.

I'm starting over right now. Recently, I sold about 75 percent of my business, which has led to some big adjustments in my life. I've spent decades focused on the goals of building and running my business. Meeting those goals took most of my time, but I developed a routine that I had become very used to. There is something comforting about knowing what to expect— going to the office, having meetings, taking business trips.

I could choose to get depressed or worried about this new start. I could take the attitude that the best times are behind me. In fact, the best times could be behind me if I decide to spend my new free time just sitting around. Instead, I'm deciding to spend more time doing charity work. Getting more involved is a new way to spend the extra time that I have. I get *excited* every time I volunteer for a good cause. And when I go to bed at the end of a day, knowing that the work I've done made someone's life a little easier or better, I can tell you that it makes for a good night's sleep.

Take that good, hard look in the mirror to see who you really are. Be honest with yourself about everything that is working for you and everything that isn't working for you. (Try to find balance—don't be too easy or too hard on yourself.) Figure out the changes you need to make to live the life you want; find the courage to make a new start as the person that *you* want to be; and make that new start full of hope and enthusiasm. I know you can do it!

EXERCISE: When You Look at Yourself,
Are You Seeing 20/20?

To do this exercise, you need a buddy. Try to choose someone who cares enough to be honest with you—if you've got a girlfriend who has the courage to tell you that an outfit makes you look too "hippy," she's the *perfect* choice.

First, answer these questions yourself and don't show your answers to your buddy.

1. In terms of your physical appearance, you:
   a. Are looking good.
   b. Need a little work in the following areas:_____
   c. Have started to let things go, most noticeably in the following areas: _____

2. Lately your moods have been:
   a. Downright sunny.
   b. Pretty balanced—mostly good with a bad day every now and then.
   c. Depressed or angry. You're focusing a lot more on what's wrong with your life instead of what's right with it.

3. As far as school or work is concerned, you're:
    a. At the top of your game.
    b. Making an effort but you could be applying yourself more.
    c. Just going through the motions. I think the problem is

    _____

4. In your romantic relationships, you're
    a. Making the most of the relationship you're in or looking for love in all the right places.
    b. Putting romance on the back burner while you focus on a different aspect of your life.
    c. Either settling for a partner who is all wrong for you or avoiding a relationship.

5. In general, you think you're:
    a. Really trying to get the most out of life.
    b. Making some effort to improve your life.
    c. Simply settling for life as it is or living in the past.

Now comes the hard part. Ask your buddy to answer the same questions about you. Remind her that you want her to be honest—and remind yourself, too. You can't get upset or angry if she tells you something you don't like. You asked!

If some of her answers are different from yours, you'll need to do some soul searching. Has she uncovered something that you weren't seeing or are her own issues clouding her vision of you? If you're not sure, you can try asking someone else to answer the same question to see if her view aligns more closely with your buddy's or yours. Consider the results as information to help you get closer in touch with who you are and who you want to be.

Some Great Resources

The Acorn Principle: Know Yourself, Grow Yourself: Discover, Explore, and Grow the Seeds of Your Greatest Potential by Jim Cathcart

Battling the Inner Dummy: The Craziness of Apparently Normal People by David Weiner and Gilbert M. Hefter

Excuse Me, Your Life Is Waiting: The Astonishing Power of Feelings by Lynn Grabhorn

Finding the Inner You: How Well Do You Know Yourself? by Dr. John Church

Girlosophy: The Oracle by Anthea Paul

12

LIGHTEN UP—AND I'M NOT JUST TALKING ABOUT THE SCALE

Laughter is a tranquilizer with no side-effects.
—ARNOLD H. GLASOW

You grow up the day you have your first real laugh—at yourself.
—ETHEL BARRYMORE

Know yourself. Don't accept your dog's admiration as conclusive evidence that you are wonderful.
—ANN LANDERS

Relax and enjoy the ride—there are no refunds.
—ANONYMOUS

THE JOURNEY INTO YOUR FUTURE is going to get very tiring if you're carrying the weight of the world with you.

This chapter is going to help you get started on the right foot by lightening up—and I'm not just talking about the scale. I'm talking about *baggage*.

For most of us, that baggage is made up of a lot of little bags full of problems, issues, and insecurities that we carry around every day until our knees are ready to buckle under the pressure. Of course, we keep meaning to get rid of those bags . . . tomorrow. Well, consider this your wake-up call—it's tomorrow!—and it's time to put some of those bags down once and for all.

The best place to start, as always, is right in front of your mirror. Ask yourself, *Hey, kiddo, what's been holding you back? What's been weighing you down? What can you change that will make you feel more lighthearted about your future?*

That kind of self-survey is easier for me to take when I look at my life one piece at a time. Since I'm already looking in the mirror, taking a look at my physical appearance is an easy place to start. I ask myself, *Am I noticing more lines in my face? Am I letting myself go when it comes to diet or exercise? Am I getting more gray hairs than I'd like to have? Is my wardrobe getting a little outdated (or sloppy or worn)? Am I looking tired because I'm not getting enough sleep?*

How You Look, How You Feel

The exact questions we choose to ask ourselves—along with answers we give—will be different for everyone because everyone's different! We all have different issues and priorities. There is no right or wrong here—only *how you feel* about your appearance.

How you look has a lot to do with how you feel. People who feel good about the way they look tend to stand a little straighter, hold their head a bit higher, and even walk with a more confident stride. If you feel good about your appearance, you tend to work harder at looking even better.

The reverse is also true. If there is one aspect of your appearance that you're unhappy with, it's easier to start ignoring other aspects of your appearance, too. When I was very overweight, I often walked around wearing blue jeans and one of my husband's old shirts. I avoided full-length mirrors like the plague.

Of course, not all overweight people lose interest in their appearance the way I did. In my business, I see a lot of people who are battling weight problems but always make the effort to look their best. My point is that when you feel bad about one part of your appearance, it's easier to let other things go, too, until one problem becomes five or ten problems.

For me, losing weight sparked my interest in wearing clothes that flattered my new figure. I started to recognize that when I look better, I just seem to feel better.

Does all this concern over physical appearance seem a bit frivolous? It's not. The truth is that physical appearance matters. That may not be fair, but it's the way life is. The wrapping on the package can excite you before you even see the gift. The first thing we see in others, and the first thing they see in us, is that outside wrapping.

When we see someone who looks vibrant, healthy, and well groomed, we're more interested in getting to know her than someone who looks tired, sloppy, and walks with slumped shoulders. None of those things tell us who is the kinder person or the smarter person or the more interesting person underneath it all. But our first impression—which, incidentally, takes less than five seconds to form in our mind—is based on how people look.

The actress Gwyneth Paltrow has never been overweight a day in her life. When she wore a fat suit to play a role in which her character was more than one hundred pounds overweight, she was appalled at how unkindly she was treated by people who didn't recognize her and who didn't know she was in costume. It's not fair, but that's the way life is.

That doesn't mean that you should base the physical changes that you want to make on what others say. You're probably not going to feel better about yourself if you become a redhead because your husband's first girlfriend had hair that color and he always thought it was the color to have. From a weight-loss perspective, studies have shown that people who try to lose weight for someone other than themselves are usually unsuccessful. If you really want to try Botox injections but your girlfriends are against the procedure, they shouldn't have it . . . but maybe you should. If your girlfriends think liposuction is a great way to get a better shape, but you hate the thought of it, then they might want to consider trying it themselves—you can stick with exercise, weight training, or loving your body just as it is.

Improve your physical appearance to lighten the baggage you carry into the future, but do it on your own terms based on what will make you feel better about you. Look into your mirror and remind yourself who you are and want you want—remember, it's *your* life.

Terry's Story

I used to see Terry once a month at the beauty salon when our appointments coincided. Terry always came in for the same thing, a trim of her short, serviceable hairstyle. Slim and with a lovely complexion, she was always neatly but plainly dressed and never wore makeup—and her thick glasses seemed to make her self-conscious. Most of the time, Terry walked looking down at the floor—but if you managed to catch her eye, she always offered a sweet smile. Sooner or later, we'd end up sitting next to each other, and I'd make it a point to strike up a conversation. Little by little, she became more comfortable talking to me and eventually, we started having regular chats during her monthly appointment.

One day, Terry came in more excited than I'd ever seen her. She said that she had just found out that she was a good candidate for surgery to correct her vision. "I could finally get rid of these!" she said, pointing at her glasses. Then her smile dimmed and she said, "But my brother-in-law told me not to have the surgery. He's a doctor and he says that something can go wrong during any surgery and that I shouldn't take unnecessary chances." I said, "Terry, are you asking me what I think you should do?" When she said that she was, I answered, "I think you should get a second opinion about whether you're a good candidate for the surgery. If that doctor agrees that you're a good candidate, then I think *you* should weigh the benefits against the risks and decide what is best for *you*. You're the only one who has to live with your glasses or the outcome of the surgery. It has to be your choice." When she left the salon that day, I could hardly wait to find out what she would decide.

As it turned out, I had to miss my next appointment. By the time I saw her again, it was two months later and I could hardly believe my eyes. Terry was sitting in the chair with a big smile on her face and no glasses. She was getting a new hairstyle that included highlights! Talking a mile a minute, she told me all about the surgery and how she could now see without her glasses. For the first time in her life, she was actually looking forward to having her picture taken for her driver's license. I was so happy for Terry . . . and more than a little curious to see if other changes would follow.

Within six months, Terry was wearing makeup every day, wearing clothes that flattered her figure, and dating a very nice man whom she had met on a blind date. Now Terry and I see each other at the salon every other week—she's coming in more often because she likes the way she looks—and I'm always thrilled to hear her latest adventures. Just think, it all started with one change. Everything changed when she decided to take charge of her life.

Examine Your Insides

Once you've surveyed your outward appearance, it's time to think about what's weighing you down on the inside. Start by looking at how you're feeling on an average day. Ask yourself how much time, on average, do you spend feeling happy? Angry? Resentful? Anxious? Sad? Stressed? Wouldn't you like to spend less time having those feelings? You may be thinking at this point, *Florine, I can't always control how I'm going to feel*. Sometimes that's true.

If a tragedy happens, we can't help but feel sad and maybe even angry. The point is that tragedies don't happen every day, yet many of us act as if they do. We sometimes blow things out of proportion, getting more upset than we should by life's everyday problems. If we're going to lighten the baggage we carry into the future, it is so important that we gain perspective about what is deadly serious and what just isn't.

How upset do you get if your computer breaks down or someone puts a dent in your car in the parking lot, or you forget that you're having company for dinner and they're coming in two hours? Take the computer to the shop, report the dent to your insurance company (that's what we have insurance for!), and order takeout and serve it on your best dishes. These are not things that are worth getting upset over. Life is too short. If this was your last day or week or month on earth, how low would these things be on your list of priorities? My guess is very low. A week from now, none of those so-called problems are going to mean anything, so why make them such a big deal now? Start getting into the habit of minimizing—instead of maximizing—life's little traumas. Make a conscious decision to downplay all the stuff that gets in your way, changing your feelings about the day from "If one more thing goes wrong, I'll just scream" to "I'm happy to be alive."

Life's Little Traumas

One of my favorite stories about life's little traumas came from my friend Sarah. Company was coming for dinner, so Sarah had spent the day doing laundry, shopping for groceries, and trying to get the house in order. Nothing was going right. She'd had to go to two supermarkets to find all the ingredients her recipes called for, she'd accidentally included her new red blouse in a load of whites (turning all of her husband's underwear pink), and the best was yet to come. Sarah was vacuuming in the hallway when she smelled the dinner rolls that she'd forgotten about burning in the oven. While she was dumping the rolls in the trash, Sarah heard awful gurgling and grinding sounds coming from the bathroom. She rushed in to find that her toddler son, Michael, had just vacuumed all the water out of the toilet. It was *not* a wet/dry vacuum. Michael looked up at her proudly and with a big smile, announced, "I helpin' Mommy."

Anyone would agree that things were not going according to plan. Sarah could have gotten really angry, she could have burst into tears, or she could have done exactly what she did—she sat down on the floor, hugged her little boy, and laughed and laughed. Maybe she laughed just a little bit hysterically . . . but she laughed. Sarah then explained to Michael—as best she could—why it's not a good idea to vacuum the potty, called her husband and asked him to pick up rolls on the way home, soaked the load of whites with some bleach, made a note to herself to go to the vacuum repair shop tomorrow, and ended up hosting a very enjoyable dinner.

Sarah was an adult—just because things weren't going her way, she couldn't burst into tears or throw a fit like, well, a toddler. And where would throwing a fit have gotten her? Where does it get any of us? Getting that upset just makes us feel worse.

Remember when you were little and your idea of a little trauma was a scraped knee? You'd call for your mother and ask her to fix it. If she was like most mommies (including mine), she'd wrap her arms around you, wipe away your tears, tell you that you were going to be just fine, put a Band-Aid on your scrape, and for that extra touch, treat you to some milk and cookies. By the time she was done, it was almost worth getting the scraped knee in the first place.

Now that you're grown up, it's up to you to fix your own little traumas. As adults, we find that our scrapes are less likely to involve knees and more likely to involve plans that go haywire, budgets that get blown, and relationships that get broken, but they're traumas for us just the same. Think about the last "scrape" you got and try to recall how you responded. Did you respond by pacing the floor, wringing your hands, and worrying until you couldn't even sleep at night? If so, what good did that do? First of all, the vast majority of things we worry about never happen anyway. Second, worry isn't going to keep something bad from happening. As the poet Maya Angelou once said, "We spend precious hours fearing the inevitable. It would be wise to use that time loving our families, being grateful for our friends and living our lives." We get only so much time in this life—there are so many better ways to spend it than worrying over things that may not happen or that we have no power to prevent.

Did you respond to that scrape with anger, taking it out on the people around you by being grouchy and short-tempered? If so, it probably didn't it help and almost certainly made the situation worse.

Did you respond with a behavior that might have made you feel good for the moment but actually made you feel much worse later? As you know, for years my solution to all of life's scrapes was a gallon of ice cream. Sure, it tasted great and felt so comforting at the time, but by the next day, whatever problem I'd been having was still there and on top of it, I felt terrible about myself. I spent more time beating myself up over eating all that ice cream than I did solving my problems. I started to get smarter when I started looking in the mirror before I had the ice cream and asked myself, *What is that ice cream going to do* for *me? How is it going to solve my problem?* Of course, there was no good answer to that. But when I asked myself, *What is that ice cream going to do* to *me?* I had lots of things to say: *Well, it's going to make my clothes fit even tighter, my face will break out, and I'll beat myself up tomorrow for eating too much.* Those talks helped me focus on taking more positive actions to cope with traumas. Talking to the mirror can help you, too.

Talk Yourself Down

Start by talking yourself down. Acknowledge everything that has just gone wrong and ask yourself how you're going to handle it. Maybe the best way to handle the problem is to deal with it head-on. Maybe right now *isn't* the time to deal with the problem. Maybe you need a cooling-off period so that you don't say or do something you'll regret later. Maybe it's a case where you don't need to deal with the problem at all and you'll be much better off to put the whole episode behind you. It's up to you to make those decisions about the best course of action—and you *can* do it.

Get into the habit of telling yourself that everything is going to be all right (instead of that everything is going to be all wrong), dust yourself off, and treat yourself to something that is going to make you feel better. Take some time at home to make your own TLC—you know the little pleasures I'm talking about, a phone call with a long-distance friend, soaking in a warm bubble bath, sipping a cup of herbal tea or a glass of wine, or snuggling with someone you love. Sometimes that's all you really need to help you see the mountains of the day as the molehills that they really are.

Happy music is wonderful TLC for life's scrapes. It's really hard to stay down when you're singing a happy song. Sing with someone you love or sing to yourself in the mirror.

Laughter is also terrific medicine for whatever is ailing you. I have some of the *I Love Lucy* shows on tape so that I can watch them whenever I need a lift. Who can watch Lucy drinking Vitameatavegamin or trying to keep up with that chocolate assembly line and not smile or even laugh out loud?

One day, I was with my husband while he was getting some tests at the hospital. I was wheeling him in the wheelchair, which was broken, and I stubbed my toe so hard that I saw stars. When I looked, I saw that the skin was broken. Bill felt so bad for me and asked what he could do. I replied that I didn't know—and tears actually started coming to my eyes. Then Bill said, "Give me your foot and I'll kiss it!" I took my sandal off, lifted my foot, and do you know what? He put his fingers to his lips and kissed them and then gently touched them to my foot. He really did kiss my toe! It was the best TLC I could have asked for. He made me feel so special and loved. Just then, a nurse walked in and said, "Exactly what are you two doing?!" When we explained, she said, "I have just the thing you need," and she put a dinosaur Band-Aid on my toe. I kept that dinosaur Band-Aid on all day. The rest of the day at the hospital got pretty tough, but every time I looked down at that dinosaur Band-Aid, I'd find myself cracking a smile. There is nothing funny about being sick or getting hurt—but you can find ways to lighten the moment.

Other Ways to Lighten Your Load

Once you've surveyed what's weighing down the inner you and the outer you, it's time to take a look at other parts of your life and other baggage you can lighten up.

Think about the relationships you have with your friends and family. Is there some long-lasting feud or tension with someone you love that is weighing you down? Are you feeling resentful because of something that a loved one said or did? Are you feeling guilty because you've been neglecting your parents, your siblings, or your children? What do you want the future of all these relationships to look like? Situations like these—and the feelings that come with them—can be some of the heaviest baggage of all. It has been my experience that ignoring them almost never makes them go away. Neither you nor your loved ones can take back harsh words or thoughtless actions, but you do have the power to decide what happens next. As the quotations writer Carl Bard said, "Though no one can go back and make a brand-new start, anyone can start from now and make a brand-new ending."

If you've been wronged, it's time to forgive and forget. Carrying around bitterness and anger can only weigh you down and rob you of future happiness. I've been married and I've been divorced. I don't remember the reasons I got divorced. I simply choose not to remember the unhappy times. I do remember the reasons I got married—I choose to remember all the things I loved about him in the first place. Making those choices is what allows exes to remain friendly and families— even in divorce—to remain a little close. That is so important, especially when there are children involved. It makes life much easier for everybody when you can truly forgive and forget. Then you can create a happier ending day by day by day.

If you've done wrong, ask for forgiveness, make amends where you can, and don't look back. You can't control whether that person forgives you. All you can do is try to make things right between the two of you and, for better or worse, turn your energies to building a happier future. Look into the mirror and remind yourself that everybody makes mistakes. Remember the formula for happy relationships. If someone is making you happy 80 percent of the time, it's worth it to overlook that other 20 percent.

If the baggage you're carrying is that you don't have friends or a love interest, you can do something about that. Start by joining clubs or volunteer groups where you can meet people who share your interests. The same is true of romantic relationships. You can't sit at home, hoping that some wonderful single person is going to coming knocking on the door looking for you. You've got to get out and meet people! Then, accept the fact that to have a relationship—whether it's friendship or something more—you've got to commit your time and effort to making the bond between the two of you grow. I think that having people I can count on—and who can count on me—is worth the time and effort it takes to form and nurture that relationship. Only you can decide if having those relationships is worth it to you.

Money Troubles

There is other personal baggage to consider. Are your finances wearing you down? So many people today are carrying personal debt that is out of control. Do you cringe every time you

TALK TO THE MIRROR

pick up the mail because you don't want to see another bill? Are you afraid to answer the phone because it might be a bill collector? Is debt something you want to carry into your future? If not, now is the time to commit to getting your finances under control.

Spend a month recording everywhere your money goes—and I mean everywhere. If you give a dollar to a children's soccer league that is camped out in front of the supermarket, record it. When you've got a month's worth of information, analyze it in terms of what is a "need" and what is a "want." Think about how you can spend your money more efficiently. Do you really need everything you're buying? Could you cut back on some items or even eliminate some spending altogether?

Prioritize your loans and credit cards by interest rate. Pay a little bit on everything and pay extra on the one with the highest interest rate. When you pay that off, target the next loan or credit card that you're going to pay off. This only works if you don't keep buying more and spending more money. One credit card is plenty for most people.

If your debt load is so out of control that you don't feel you can fix it yourself, contact a nonprofit credit and debt counseling organization that specializes in helping people get out of debt. They will help you consolidate your debt, negotiate lower interest rates with your creditors, and help you learn how to manage your money more effectively.

Consider having a yard sale or a garage sale. You'll enter your future with less clutter and some quick cash when you get rid of the things you no longer use or want.

Create a budget and make sure that it includes a line item for savings. Too often, people don't include savings in their budgets. Establish a savings account and put a set amount of money in it every time you get paid before you pay anyone else. Then you won't have to worry about where the money will

196

come from to pay for unexpected or emergency expenses. That's a big piece of baggage to unload!

What's Your Calling?

We still haven't talked about your professional future. Are you happy doing the work you do? Is there other work that you'd rather be doing? If you're a stay-at-home mom, would you rather work outside the home, even part time? If you work outside the home, would you rather be a stay-at-home mom? Have you ever dreamed of starting your own business or going back to school?

Unfulfilled dreams can really weigh you down. You don't want to wake up at 50 or 60 or 70 or 80 or even 100, saying, "If only . . ." If only I had done this, if only I had done that. Regret is a terrible thing. *Now* is the time to plan and act on that plan so that you don't wake up one day and say to yourself, "If only . . ." Don't be afraid that you might be making a mistake to take your future in a direction. If the first plan doesn't work out, remember you can always make a new plan.

I have a friend who volunteers at a drug and alcohol rehabilitation clinic where she befriended a woman named Denise. To be candid, Denise had made a real mess of the first thirty years of her life. She was a single parent who had a high school diploma but had no job. She had developed a drug and alcohol problem. Over time, she started to realize that at the rate she was going, her life would probably end very soon. This was not the legacy that she wanted to leave her daughter, so she made a hard decision. She left her daughter with her ex-mother-in-law. She didn't know how or when she'd be back.

The first plan that Denise made was to get sober. She checked herself into a drug treatment facility and joined Alcoholics Anonymous. Denise made a real commitment to working both programs, and she did, day by day by day. After several months, she was able to break her alcohol and drug habits. Denise's next plan was to find a job (plus a second job!) to save money so that she could go back to school. After one year of working seventy hours a week, every week, Denise managed to save about 25 percent of the money she needed for school while still sending money to her ex-mother-in-law for her daughter's care. She started applying for scholarships and won one—enough to go to school to become a licensed practical nurse. When she completed the program, she found work at a hospital, rented an apartment, and with her ex-mother-in-law's blessing, took her daughter with her to start their new life together.

Today Denise is completing her degree to become a registered nurse and plans to one day become a nurse anesthetist. Her ex-mother-in-law comes over once a week for dinner—Denise and she have become very close. Does she regret her past? Of course. But she doesn't allow herself to dwell on it. She is too busy making the most of her future. Was giving up drugs and alcohol easy for Denise? No—breaking those habits was the hardest thing she had ever done. Working two jobs and going back to school was also tough. But she made a commitment to changing the end of her story and maybe changing her daughter's story as well. She changed her future one day at a time and you can, too. Just keep trying. Look into that mirror every single day and remind yourself what you want for yourself and those are around you.

Abraham Lincoln was right when he said, "Most folks are about as happy as they make up their minds to be." Make up your mind to be happy—to smile—as much and as often as you can. Find happy ways to feel better about life's scrapes, and the baggage you carry into your future will be so much lighter.

The future is *yours*—yours to build the life you've always wanted—but you've got to be committed to doing what it takes. It doesn't just happen—it's hard work. Remember, to be successful, you've got to first decide what you want and then decide what you're willing to do to get it. Now is the time to unload the baggage that's been holding you back so that you can create the future of your dreams.

SELF-TEST: A Suitcase, a Steamer Trunk, or a Cargo Hold—How Much Baggage Have You Got?

1. How happy are you with your physical appearance?
   a. I love the way I look.
   b. Nobody is perfect, but I'm pretty comfortable in my own skin.
   c. There are at least three or four areas that I'd like to improve.
   d. I dislike more about my looks than I like.

2. If someone made a movie about your life, it would be:
   a. A comedy—things are pretty upbeat around here.
   b. An action film—busy but exciting.
   c. A drama—things get pretty serious.
   d. A tragedy—have a box of tissues in hand.

3. When you think about your family and friends, how healthy are your relationships?
   a. Pretty healthy. We don't have too many issues, but when we do, we talk honestly about them to resolve the problem.
   b. Sometimes a little tension builds up, but we usually put it behind us.
   c. In at least a few of my relationships, we hold things in that are bothering us. Then they come out later as sarcastic comments or jibes.
   d. I'm estranged from some of my family or longtime friends.

4. How is your financial health?
   a. I'm a saver and a bargain hunter. If I don't have the money for something I want, I don't buy it.
   b. I have a loan and/or a credit card but payment is never an issue. I put money in savings every month.
   c. I'm making ends meet, but I live pretty much paycheck to paycheck.
   d. I'm overextended, considering bankruptcy, or have recently declared bankruptcy.

5. Describe the work you do.
   a. It provides enough money and enriches my life. I enjoy the work I do every day.
   b. My job is a stepping stone to the job I really want— but I'm enjoying the journey it takes to get there.
   c. My job is simply a way to make my personal life more enjoyable. The work itself means nothing to me.
   d. I hate my job or get sick at the thought of going to work.

Analysis

Scoring this self-test is fairly self-explanatory. You can look at the options and see that a's are much more desirable than d's. But knowing what your answer should be and what answer really applies to your life are two different things. Be honest with yourself.

Having a's and b's mean that your baggage is pretty light. You're in great shape to make the most of your future. C's are a sign that you could be getting a bit overloaded in certain areas. You might want to consider some adjustments. If you circled a d under *any* question, you may be about to buckle from the weight of the baggage you're carrying. Take a look at what you need to unload and deal with the problem or problems head on. Your future awaits!

EXERCISE: Dare to Dream

Write a few sentences—a paragraph at most—to describe the life you would like to be living in five years. (Remember, we're talking about dreams here—not fantasy. You can want to be the queen of England, but I don't think she's going to abdicate the throne.) Start with the life you're living now and dream up the best possible outcomes. You don't have to address every possible aspect of your life. Just write down the first things that come to your mind.

Reread those sentences. Most likely, you are looking at your own priorities because they were the first dreams that came to your mind. Take a look at the baggage we uncovered in this chapter and think about which bags are holding you back from the dreams you most want to realize. Unload those bags first. The secret of getting ahead is getting started.

Some Great Resources

Fish!: A Remarkable Way to Boost Morale and Improve Results by Stephen C. Lundin

Freedom from the Ties That Bind: The Secret of Self Liberation by Guy Finley

How to Forgive Yourself and Others: Steps to Reconciliation by Eamon Tobin

Look Who's Laughing by Ann Spangler and Shari Macdonald

Second Thoughts On: How to Be as Terrific as Your Dog Thinks You Are! by Mort Crim

The Secret of Letting Go by Guy Finley

13

Don't Get Older — Get Bolder

You are young at any age if you are planning for tomorrow.
—Anonymous

You're never too old to become younger.
—Mae West

I want to die young at an advanced age.
—Max Lerner

Don't turn this page! Forgive me for shouting, but I had to get the attention of some of you twenty- and thirty-year-olds, along with the rest of us, who think this chapter might not apply to you. The fact is we are all aging—although some of us have been doing it longer than others. And yes, it's true, there is no way to stop time from marching on.

But it's important to realize that we still have choices about *how* we age. Whether we're thirty, eighty, or somewhere in between, we make decisions that impact our physical and mental health, as well as our emotional well-being. In short, *you* decide how *you're* going to feel.

That's why I remind myself every morning when I talk to the mirror to build more happy times into the day. I've only got so much time in this world, so I want to fill that time with as many good moments as I can. I want to spend the time I'm given having the time of my life.

I play tennis with a man who just turned ninety, and I'm not embarrassed to say that he gives me a run for my money on the tennis court. If that surprises you, then this will amaze you. He also still goes to work every day, takes walks on a treadmill three times a week, and he just published a novel. He has a daily agenda for all the things that he wants and needs to do, and he goes out and accomplishes them. He is always looking forward to tomorrow with great enthusiasm and a twinkle in his eye. Instead of living in the past, he is living today to the fullest and dreaming of his future. He believes in making his dreams come true and he truly loves his life.

When Age Is More than Just a Number

You may have noticed that in my own story I never mentioned my age. I'm a little sensitive about aging because although it's just a number, your age can affect how some people treat you.

I saw a very disturbing example of just how true that is at a party I went to last year. There was a beautiful, vibrant blonde there visiting from California named Gloria. She had it all going for her. In addition to her good looks, she owned her own business, had a great sense of humor, and could speak intelligently on a variety of subjects. She was a good listener and had a flair for making the people around her feel comfortable. It's not surprising that Gloria was surrounded by eligible men at this party—most of whom I knew to be in their late forties. The party was in full swing when I overheard one of them say, "I sure wish you lived here, Gloria, because I'd love to take you out." Some of the other men also chimed in, saying they'd like to date her, too. Then Gloria said, "That would be so terrific because back in California, I just can't seem to get a date." They were shocked. One man even asked her how that could be when she was so good-looking. Gloria replied, "Well, once they find out that I'm almost seventy, no one asks me out." It got very quiet for a moment. The conversation started back up again, but, one by one, those men made their excuses and disappeared from Gloria's side. Her looks didn't go away, her engaging personality didn't change, her sense of humor remained the same, but now she was labeled as old.

What happened to Gloria wasn't right and it certainly wasn't fair—but that's the way life seems to be. I don't think that these guys were exceptions to the rule—they *were* the rule. Many people who have no prejudices about race, gender, or religion still unconsciously discriminate against age. Think about it. If I told you that I was sixty-five or seventy-five or eighty-five, you might begin to think of me as a different person. You might put me in a box that is marked with your preconceptions of people who are "my age." That box might say things like, "Senior citizen with dull, thinning hair, sagging skin, tired and retired, wears sensible shoes and uses a walker, out of date, past her prime."

The worst thing about that box is that it becomes so easy to climb in. All of a sudden, people start treating you differently. They want to take your hand when you're crossing the street. They want to help you get up from a chair. You're no different, but they start treating you differently. Soon you start thinking, *Oh my God, I really am getting older.* Your shoulders start to round, you start walking with your head down, and you find yourself in the same routine day after day until life becomes one old, boring rut. And the only difference between a rut and a grave is the depth.

Choose Your Age

I believe life should be exciting every single day. Age shouldn't have anything to do with how much enthusiasm you have for life.

People don't wish you a "Happy Birth*year*"; they say, "Happy Birth*day*!" so celebrate every birthday as the wonderful event it is. Your birthday marks the day you were given the gift of this life. That's worth celebrating no matter how few or how many candles are on your cake.

Three of the most damaging words in the English language are *act your age*. I decide the age I'm going to act. One year I decided to be forty. That wasn't a very good year for me so the next year I decided to be forty-three. That was a terrific year so I've decided to stick with it. On my birthday, I'm forty-three—every time. Not only do I tell people that I'm forty-three, I act and think as if I'm that age. To help me stay forty-three on the inside, I maintain a healthy weight, exercise regularly, and eat at least five servings of fruits and vegetables and drink six to eight glasses of water every day. To stay forty-three on the outside, I color my hair, wear my hair at a longer, more youthful length, and keep my wardrobe looking fashionable.

You can make the same choice. Take a look in the mirror and decide the age you want to be—then think, act, dress, and most of all, *live* your chosen age with real enthusiasm!

Joan's Story

I have a very good friend named Joan who many years ago was widowed at the age of forty. After about a year, Joan began dating again, but her prominent, conservative family was scandalized when she started dating men who were younger than she was. Family members decided to find a husband for her that they felt would be more suitable. It wasn't long before they fixed her up with Robert, a successful businessman. When she learned that Robert was fifty, ten years older than she was, she was hesitant, but decided what the heck, she'd go out with him. It was a perfect match. They fell in love, married, and had thirty wonderful years together. Robert treated Joan like a queen and Joan treated Robert like a king. They both lived active lifestyles—by the time Joan was seventy, Robert (at eighty!) was still right by her side doing all the things they loved to do—socializing, working, and traveling. The night before their annual vacation to Europe, Robert died in his sleep. Joan was devastated. I went to their home to pay my respects and found her in a state of shock. Because Robert's death had been so sudden, I wasn't surprised. But when Joan explained the nature of her shock, I was a little shocked myself. Robert had always taken care of their finances so she never looked at their legal documents. When he died, however, the funeral home wanted his birth certificate, so she got it from the safe. "Florine," she said, "Robert wasn't eighty when he died—he was ninety!"

We realized immediately why Robert had lied about his age. Joan's family knew that Robert was right for her, but they also knew that she would never give him a chance if she knew that he was sixty when she was only forty. So Robert always lived ten years younger than he was. He behaved ten years younger, thought of himself as ten years younger, and essentially *became* ten years younger.

Life Starts Now!

Life doesn't start later. It doesn't start *after* you lose the weight or *after* you get a better job or *after* your mother or your kids start appreciating you. It starts right now, my friend! Right now is all we've got, so how can we make this moment the best? You're hurting yourself and those around you by not living to your potential. It's your job to have that zest for living almost every single day, and if you don't—shame on you. It's time to take a good look in the mirror and start talking!

You're not going to grow ten years younger in a day. You didn't age ten years in a day, either. But instead of being so focused on aging, shift that focus as you talk to the mirror and *decide* to grow younger. Our culture is already redefining what growing older means. It's up to you to redefine it for *you.*

If you think about it, not long ago people viewed retirement as sitting in a rocking chair daydreaming about the past. Today most people who retire at sixty-two or older go on to whole new professions or pursuits. It can be the best time in your life—a time to live your dreams. You've got knowledge, experience, and the freedom to focus. You are *hot*—you are in the moment. *Stretch* those undeveloped abilities, search out new experiences, and go forward. After all, your brain is like the rest of your body—use it or lose it.

It's Never Too Late—or Too Early

That's the way that Molly Leonelli, another Remarkable Woman, lives every day. Molly is the president of a company that blends industrial chemicals for international clients in the metal-finishing industry. As busy as her business keeps her, she makes time in her agenda for regular workouts at a local athletic club, attending cultural events (especially opera!), managing her stocks, and keeping up with the financial newspapers and magazines that she loves to read. When she takes a vacation, Molly likes to travel . . . Europe, Alaska, China—you name it and Molly has probably been there. And did I mention that Molly happens to be ninety years old?

When I asked her to share the secrets of her longevity, Molly was happy to oblige. She says, "I always maintain a healthy diet and exercise regularly, and I never drink or smoke, so that I have the energy to carry out the goals I set for myself every day. As long as I have goals to achieve—things to do that really matter to me—I have a reason to keep active. It's that physical and mental activity that keeps people young."

Molly has lived a lifetime of good health and goal-setting, but if you haven't, it's never too late to start. Jean was sixty-two years old when she retired from her job because her emphysema was getting the best of her. She'd given up smoking, but she just didn't have the energy to continue working anymore. It was a very depressing time for Jean—she saw her future as sitting in front of the TV waiting for life to be over. A friend convinced Jean to go to a Weight Watchers meeting. She had put on a lot of weight when she gave up cigarettes and had tried several diets to take the weight off without any success. Still, she felt that if she could manage to lose as little as twenty pounds, she might be able to breathe a little easier. When Jean went to her first meeting, she weighed in at 240 pounds. She listened to the details of the plan, but by the end of the meeting, she still wasn't feeling terribly inspired. She promised herself to give it a week, just to see what would happen. To Jean's surprise, she lost four pounds—a substantial loss—so she thought she'd try it a little longer.

Jean wrote to me six months later—after she reached her goal weight of 153 pounds! Her letter said, "When I reached my goal, I found that I no longer suffered terribly with my emphysema. I've decided to live my dream of seeing America. I've bought an RV, and I'm on a nine-week trip with two cats and two dogs as my traveling companions. I'm having the time of my life! I never thought this could happen to me—I've taken my life back! I've taken charge!"

You can take charge of your life, too. Just look in the mirror and tell yourself what you want.

Just as Jean found that it's never too late to start living younger, it's also never too early. Dana confesses to her friend Janice that she's put on five pounds. Janice, who is trying to be comforting, says, "Well, you know we're thirty now. We're just not going to be able to maintain the weight we did when we were twenty." That's not true of course, but it's so comforting to think that someone or something else (not us!) could be responsible for our weight gain. Dana grabs onto this rationalization like a drowning woman grabbing a life preserver. A few days later, when Dana is feeling too tired to get up and exercise, Janice's words come back to her and now she applies them to exercise. *Now that I'm thirty, I'm just not going to have the energy I had at twenty,* she thinks and climbs back into bed. Soon, Dana's five added pounds become ten, ten become twenty, twenty become . . . well, you get the picture.

Dana's one little rationalization grew into one big self-fulfilling prophecy. She used aging as an excuse, she acted as if she was aging, and now she's getting old before her time.

Don't get old—stay active just as long as you can. When it's time for God to take you, be the most surprised of anyone. Live your life every day that you're alive!

SELF-TEST: Are You Ready to Rock or
Ready for the Rocker?

1. When was the last time you updated your hairstyle?
   a. Within the last few months—I like to experiment with new looks.
   b. A year or two ago.
   c. I can't remember the last time I made a change.

2. When it comes to fashion you:
   a. Watch the trends and have some new styles in your closet.
   b. Know what the new fashions look like, but can't say you own any.
   c. Are still wearing looks from ten years ago.

3. The last time I tried something totally new was:
   a. Within the last month.
   b. Within the last several months.
   c. A year ago or more.

4. When you look at people your age, would you say you:
   a. Look and/or act younger.
   b. Look and/or act about the same age.
   c. Look and/or act older.

5. At dinner out with your friends, the most likely topic of conversation would be:
   a. Your latest projects, plans, or goals.
   b. Small talk about current events.
   c. The past or comparing aches and pains.

6. You engage in a physical activity to stay healthy and strong:
   a. At least every other day.
   b. Irregularly.
   c. Rarely or never.

7. If asked, you tell someone your dreams for the future:
   a. Immediately.
   b. It would take some thought.
   c. Not at all. I'm past that.

Analysis

Mostly a's: You're ready to rock!

Mostly b's: You're starting to show signs of a downhill slide. It's time to talk to the mirror about setting some new goals.

Mostly c's: Yikes! There is still time to reinvent your life—get up out of that rocker and live while you still can! Go back and look at the A answers and start thinking about changes you would like to make. Start small, give yourself those four months you need to make a change part of your life, and start growing younger. You can do it!

Some Great Resources

Grow Younger, Live Longer: Ten Steps to Reverse Aging by Deepak Chopra

If Not Now, When? by Stephanie Marston

It's Only Too Late If You Don't Start Now: How to Create Your Second Life at Any Age by Barbara Sher

The New Ourselves, Growing Older: Women Aging With Knowledge and Power by Diana Laskin Siegal

Stretching Lessons: The Daring that Starts from Within by Sue Bender

Strong Women Stay Young by Miriam Nelson

What's Next?: Women Redefining Their Dreams in the Prime of Life by Rena Pederson

. . .

If you have access to the Internet at home, you'll find a visit to these Web sites very helpful. If you don't have Internet access, you can use your local library's system for free. And if you don't know how to surf the Net, taking a course could be a rewarding goal to set for yourself. If you can't find a course in your area, call the local high school and tell them what you're looking for. Odds are they can hook you up with an Internet-savvy teenager!

www.florineonline.com

This is my personal Web site designed to help you live life to the fullest. Check it out often to find tips on travel, health and fitness, family, career, recipes, and an e-mail site where you can send me your questions.

www.beeson.org

This Web site offers a "Living to 100 Life Expectancy Calculator" along with lessons on feeling you best at any age. The quiz asks you to answer several questions about your lifestyle and family history. The results include your current life expectancy and changes you can make (some as easy as flossing your teeth) to increase your life expectancy and improve the quality of your life now.

www.realage.com

At this site you can take a test to assess your real age—that is, the age you are based on your health and lifestyle rather than the number of years you have lived. You can find answers to improve your quality of life, information on a wide range of health concerns and conditions, and the Real Age Tip of the Day—daily advice offered free to increase your health and decrease your "real age."

14

LIVING WELL IS THE BEST REWARD

Never regret. If it's good, it's wonderful.
If it's bad, it's experience.
—VICTORIA HOLT

Go out on a limb—that's where the fruit is.
—JIMMY CARTER

It's a funny thing about life; if you refuse to accept
anything but the very best, you very often get it.
—W. SOMERSET MAUGHAM

WERE YOU EXPECTING THAT saying to end with a different R word, like maybe . . . *revenge?* I know that's how the old saying goes, but I think that we can do better. If the desire for revenge is part of your life, it means that you're focusing on some time in the past when you were wronged and that you've got anger in your heart. To truly make the most of the future, we've got to keep looking ahead at all the wonderful possibilities—at everything that still *can* be—with a hopeful heart. We can't afford to waste time and energy on what should have been or what shouldn't have been. In the words of the actress and singer Eva Jessye, "Wear the past like a loose garment; take it off and let it drop."

Jackie's Story

If you think you can't let go of the past, that whatever happened to you was just too painful, consider the story of Remarkable Woman Jackie Pflug. In 1985 Jackie was a passenger on EgyptAir Flight 648 when the plane was hijacked. Jackie watched the terrorists execute four other passengers before it was her turn. She was shot in the head, thrown out of the plane onto the runway, and left for dead. She laid there for five hours until airport personnel came to remove her from the tarmac. When they rolled her body over on the way to the morgue, she gasped for breath and they rushed her to the hospital. Jackie suffered extensive brain damage, losing most of her sight, hearing, and short-term memory. Doctors told her that she would never work again, never drive a car again, and never read above a third-grade level. Jackie describes herself as being full of hatred for the hijackers and drowning in her own depression. Her husband and she divorced three years later.

Jackie began therapy and in time made a commitment to herself to someday smile a genuine smile and become a whole person again. Two years after making that commitment, she regained her driver's license. Four years later, she went back to work as a motivational speaker and fourteen year later, she tested at a twelfth-grade reading level.

Jackie says there were two keys to her success. The first was that she'd made a commitment to heal: "You have to have a commitment to your goals—whatever those goals may be—to keep you going when obstacles come up along the way." The second key was to let go of her bitterness and desire for revenge. The hijacker who had shot Jackie was still alive—and is, in fact, still alive today. Jackie wanted him to suffer every bit as much as she was suffering. But those negative desires were standing in her way of re-creating herself and finding happiness in the future. "It's hard to smile when your heart is full of hatred," said Jackie.

Gradually, Jackie was able to give herself what she calls the gift of forgiveness. While she still held the hijackers accountable for their actions, she was able to let go of her desire for revenge and turn to her future. Jackie remarried a few years later and today has a five-year-old son who is the joy of her life. She tours the country as a motivational speaker, giving hope and inspiration to others who have suffered at the hands of others. Jackie says that "Good always comes from what appears to be bad as long as you're willing to turn to the future and never give up."

Jackie was smart enough to see that her desire for revenge was only hurting herself. As the old proverb that says, "The fire of anger only burns the angry." Whatever wrongs have been done to you, now is the time to free yourself by letting them go.

Jackie's vengeful feelings were directed at people—the hijackers, who by the end of the siege were responsible for the deaths of fifty-nine people and Jackie's severe brain injury. But sometimes our bitterness isn't directed at people but at fate. Maybe your home was destroyed by a tornado, a hurricane, or a flood. Maybe someone you love contracted a serious illness. Maybe you were born with a physical disability. In those cases, there is no one to blame—but dwelling on what life might have been like if these things hadn't happened doesn't help anything and, just as if fate were a person, holds us back from making the most of the future.

Let Your Bitterness Go

Talk to the mirror about bitter feelings that you're holding inside. Start by saying out loud the names of everyone you feel bitter toward and what exactly he or she did to you. The more names or episodes you can name, the more anger you have holding you back from a rewarding future. When you've named every person and painful memory you can think of, say to yourself, *All this anger I'm holding inside isn't hurting them. It's hurting me—and I've been hurt enough. I refuse to give those people and painful memories control over my life. I am giving myself the gift of letting go of these memories and all the pain that goes with them. I deserve to be happy. I forgive the people who have wronged me, and I'm going to forget the pain of the past so that I can remember the good.*

If you've made a habit of dwelling on these hurtful memories, that habit (like all habits) will take time and effort to break. Every time those memories come into your mind, say, "Stop!" to yourself (out loud, if necessary). Go look into the mirror and replace that bad thought with a pleasant mental picture—a happy memory, your favorite vacation spot, *anything* that will redirect your thoughts in a positive way. Talk to yourself about those happy memories and let them fill your being until they crowd out all the things that are better forgotten.

Instead of asking why (why did this have to happen to me?), start asking why not, which, as the author Mason Cooley said, is "the slogan for an interesting life." There is no telling what you can accomplish when you use your energies to make

216

the most of the future instead of dwelling on what could have been, should have been, or never can be now.

I once heard someone say that a vengeful heart is like a prison we build for ourselves and we're the only ones who hold the key. I'm not saying this will be easy—breaking a habit is never easy—but I'm saying that you and I are worth the effort it takes to be free of painful pasts.

Talk to the Mirror to Reap the Rewards

So if we're going to change the end of the saying from *revenge* to *reward*, how do we go about living well to get those rewards? Well, that's really what our talk and this book have been all about—talking to the mirror to see your path to life's rewards more clearly.

The journey toward getting that more rewarding life begins—and continues—with talking to the mirror. That's where you'll find the friend who will always listen to what you have to say and will never tire of the conversation . . . the friend who definitely won't walk out on you. Have you stopped beating the daylights out of her? Have you started treating her with the love, care, and respect that she deserves? If you answered yes to both questions, then I couldn't be happier for you. But if you can't honestly say yes quite yet, that's okay, just *keep talking*. It doesn't really matter how long it takes to make friends with the person in the mirror—that friendship will come in its own time. What does matter is that day by day by day, you use those talks to gain a better understanding and appreciation for who you are, what's been holding you back, and what you can do to start living the life you want.

Until our next talk, live well, laugh often, love much, and feel great about yourself each and every day.

EXERCISE: Talk the Talk and Walk the Walk

This exercise works in two ways. First, it's a review of some of the strategies we've talked about along the way—strategies that have helped me to build a more rewarding life every day and that can do the same for you. Second, if you need some ideas for your next talk with the mirror, this list can help you get started.

Talk to the mirror about:

1. Setting priorities. What would be important to you if this was your last day (or week or month) on earth? How would you want to spend that time? What things seem important now but wouldn't be so important anymore? In the face of these answers, what changes should you consider making in your life now?

2. Scheduling an hour of time for yourself every day and what you can do during that time to make your days more joyful.

3. Delegating tasks to others.

4. Expecting to be treated with the same kindness that you show to others. Are you getting enough recognition from your loved ones for the loving things you do? If not, it's time to ask for it. Pats on the back and thank-yous are the sustenance of life.

5. Giving yourself the same kindness (and when necessary, forgiveness) that you give others.

6. Evaluating your relationships using the 70/30 formula.

7. Making decisions based on what works for and is right for you, instead of based on what "they" say you should be doing.

8. Deciding what exactly you want and what you're willing to give up to get it.

9. Changing the things you don't like about yourself (that you can change). If you always do what you've always done, you're always going to get what you've always gotten. What's the first change you want to make?

10. Replacing bad habits with good habits. Remember, it will take at least four months before you own a new habit!

11. Making the best of a bad choice. Ask yourself what went wrong, what damage control you can do now, and what you can do better or differently in the future.

12. Thinking and acting more positively about life's curveballs. If things aren't going your way, ask what you are going to do about it.

13. Starting to look at the tasks you have to do as opportunities instead of burdens.

14. Getting organized at home, at work, or both.

15. Making a daily agenda.

16. Responding in a positive way when love hurts. Did you take out your bad day on someone you love? Did he take out his bad day on you? Is someone you love suffering? What is the best course of action you can take now for him and for you?

17. Taking control of your own health. Make and keep appointments with your doctors. Get regular health screenings. Reach and maintain a healthy weight. Make exercise a regular part of your life. Get enough rest.

18. Lightening up the emotional baggage you're carrying.

19. Seeing yourself more clearly by putting your assets and your flaws into perspective.

20. Knowing when you need to start over (with your relationships, weight, career, etc.).

21. Living every day you're alive. Are there things you've always wanted to do but put off doing? If so, the time you have for certain is right now so you'd better get started!

22. Deciding to grow younger instead of older. I think I'll be forty-three today—how old do you want to be?

23. Choosing coping skills that will make you feel better, not worse, about yourself. Take it from me—having a warm bath and watching a funny movie are much better choices than eating a half gallon of ice cream.

24. Letting go of old hurts that are holding you back from a happy future.

25. Setting goals to accomplish every single day.

Now comes the "walk-the-talk" part. Make a plan to move forward with whatever you've been talking to the mirror about. Then take action, give yourself a time limit, and monitor your progress. If you find that the plan isn't working or you change your mind, go back to the mirror and make a new plan.

It has been said that there is only one success . . . to be able to live life in your own way. That is the success I wish for you.

Some Great Resources

Fearless Living: Live Without Excuses and Love Without Regret by Rhonda Britten

Miles to Go Before I Sleep: My Grateful Journey Back from the Hijacking of EgyptAir Flight 648 by Jackie Nink Pflug

NOTES TO MYSELF
AND
MY PERSONAL AGENDA

As I was writing down my ideas for *Talk to the Mirror*, I thought, wouldn't it be nice for my readers to have a place to write down their own ideas, too? That's why I added this section. "Notes to Myself" lists key ideas as questions for each chapter, and there is space to write down your thoughts and feelings about how these ideas might apply to your own life. They make great topics for your daily talk to the mirror, too!

Back in chapter 2, I said that I believe everyone—no matter what their age or occupation—should keep a daily agenda. Every night before I go to bed, I take a few minutes to write my agenda—a to-do list that helps me stay on track—so that I can get the things done that I have to do *and* work in more of the things that I want to do. The "Personal Agendas" I've included here are sample pages to help you get started writing your own to-do lists. Each agenda has one focus point for you to consider as you put your to-do list together for the day. You can use the personal agendas in any order, choosing a different focus each day or repeating one focus point for sixteen weeks as part of a commitment to start a great new habit—whatever works for you.

I suggest you photocopy the "Notes to Myself" and "My Personal Agenda" pages and save them in a binder. After six months of talking to the mirror, take a look at how you're managing your days. I think you'll see some real positive changes in how you decide to spend the gift of each day *and* in how you feel about your very best friend . . . you.

Chapter 2. There's a Reason They Call It the Present

Notes to Myself

Some food for thought . . . and for talking to the mirror

Who are the people and what are the things that really matter to me?

What have I been dwelling on that if today were my last day would no longer be important?

What did I learn from my "Things I Like about Me/Things I Don't Like about Me *That I Can Change*" list?

What plans can I make and carry out to get more out of each day?

My Personal Agenda

Focus: I've been given the gift of today—sixteen waking hours—and it's up to me to decide how to spend them. What activities can I plan to make the most of this time?

Chapter 3. Where Does the River Go for a Drink?

Notes to Myself

Some food for thought . . . and for talking to the mirror

What are some things I can do to recharge my battery?

Who can I ask for help with the large and small tasks or problems I have?

What tasks can I delegate to someone else?

What activities can I cut back on or cut out because I'm too busy?

How am I going to say "no" the next time my agenda is too full to say "yes"?

What plans can I make and carry out to make more time for me?

My Personal Agenda

Focus: When will I take that hour for me and what will I do with it?

Chapter 4. The Golden Rule Gets a Makeover

Notes to Myself

Some food for thought . . . and for talking to the mirror

What am I doing or saying to others that I wouldn't want them to do or say to me?

What am I allowing others to do or say to me that I wouldn't do or say to them?

Using the 70/30 Rule, are there relationships in my life that need some changes?

What changes can I make to be as kind and forgiving to myself as I am to others?

What plans can I make and carry out to put all three sides of the Golden Triangle to work in my life?

My Personal Agenda

Focus: If I knew I had only one week (or month or year) left, what would I wish I had spent more time/less time doing?

Chapter 5. Just Being Me

Notes to Myself

Some food for thought . . . and for talking to the mirror

What are some life experiences that I'd like to learn more about?

What are some practical ways for me to gain those experiences?

What fears am I allowing to hold me back from becoming the person I want to be?

Am I living my life in ways that I honestly feel are right for me, and if not, what plans can I make and carry out to make lasting changes?

My Personal Agenda

Focus: What priorities can I set to get closer to the me I want to be?

Chapter 6. C-H-A-N-G-E—for Some People, It's a Four-Letter Word

Notes to Myself

Some food for thought . . . and for talking to the mirror

What is the single most important change I could make to feel better about myself each and every day?

What has been holding me back from making that change?

What plans can I make and carry out that will enable me to make that change every day for sixteen weeks until it becomes a habit?

My Personal Agenda

Focus: When will I schedule the change I've decided to practice every single day?

Chapter 7. There's a Whole Lotta Choices Goin' On

Notes to Myself

Some food for thought . . . and for talking to the mirror

Are there choices I've been putting off because I'm afraid of making the wrong choice? If the answer is "yes," what are those choices? How can the step-by-step instructions for decision making help me move forward?

When I've made a choice that didn't turn out the way I'd planned, how can I:
    Figure out what went wrong
    Do damage control
    Apply what I've learned
    Make a plan for a better choice

My Personal Agenda

Focus: When I think about each item on my to-do list, have I made the best choices for me?

Chapter 8. How to Beat the Blues

Notes to Myself

Some food for thought . . . and for talking to the mirror

What are the messages I send myself that I need to change from "I can't" to "I can"?

What messages can I give myself to stay positive when things aren't going my way?

Who are the positive people in my life, and how can I spend more time with them?

What plans can I make and carry out that will help me the next time I get the blues?

My Personal Agenda

Focus: How can I put a positive spin on each task I have to accomplish?

Chapter 9. Take the Distress out of Stress

Notes to Myself

Some food for thought . . . and for talking to the mirror

What are the good stressors in my life (the positive energy that makes good things happen)?

How can I get more organized at home and at work to reduce my negative stress?

How can I change my daily agenda (the items on it or how I keep it) to reduce my negative stress?

What do I tend to worry about that is beyond my control? What can I do to distract myself or change my thought patterns when I start to worry about these things?

What plans can I make and carry out that will help me recover from a stressful day?

My Personal Agenda

Focus: When and how can I schedule some time to de-stress?

Chapter 10. When Love Hurts

Notes to Myself

Some food for thought . . . and for talking to the mirror

How can I respond better when loved ones take out their anger or frustrations on me?

What can I do to prevent or stop myself from taking out my anger or frustrations on my loved ones?

Am I holding on to a grudge against a friend or family member and, if I am, what can I do to heal the relationship?

What can I do to help someone I love who is sick or broken-hearted?

What plans can I make and carry out to spend more time with the people I love?

My Personal Agenda

Focus: How can I schedule more time with the people I love?

Chapter 11. Mirror, Mirror on the Wall, Am I Seeing Me at All?

Notes to Myself

Some food for thought . . . and for talking to the mirror

Am I putting off making changes that I need to make to feel better about myself?

Am I dwelling too much on certain areas or blowing flaws out of proportion?

What plans can I make and carry out for a new beginning in my life?

My Personal Agenda

Focus: What activity can I add to my agenda to make a fresh new start?

Chapter 12. Lighten Up—and I'm Not Just Talking about the Scale

Notes to Myself

Some food for thought . . . and for talking to the mirror

Am I carrying extra "baggage" that is weighing me down? Examples:

> Too much weight
>
> Worry
>
> Anger or resentment

What can I do when I'm having a bad day that will make me feel better and be good for me?

Is there an unfulfilled dream that's weighing me down? If so, what plans can I make and carry out to make that dream a reality?

My Personal Agenda

Focus: What activities can I add—or delete—to lighten the baggage in my life?

Chapter 13. Don't Get Older—Get Bolder

Notes to Myself

Some food for thought . . . and for talking to the mirror

How do I feel about the idea of getting older? What do I picture my life to be like?

What age would I like to be and what life changes can I make to live that age now?

Is there a new career or hobby I'd like to try in the next stage of my life?

What plans can I make and carry out to be the best I can be at any age?

My Personal Agenda

Focus: What activities can I add to my to-do list that will keep me young and living in the moment?

Chapter 14. Living Well Is the Best Reward

Notes to Myself

Some food for thought . . . and for talking to the mirror

Are there painful memories from my past that I'm holding on to?

How can I give myself "the gift of forgiveness"?

What plans can I make and carry out to keep me focused on all that's good in my life?

My Personal Agenda

Focus: When will I schedule a talk with the mirror today?

INDEX

talking to the mirror *(continued)*
  beating the blues, 121
  choice and, 108–110, 117
  disagreements and, 60
  freedom to make mistakes, 63
  to stop negative stress, 133,
    142, 144
  "What about me?", 57
  worry management, 141
tests. *See* questionnaires, exercises, and self-tests
"Things I Don't Like about Me
  That I Can Change" list,
  30–31, 33
  plan for things you can
    change, 31
"Things I Like about Me" list,
  30–31
thinking outside the box, 73
time for yourself
  agenda's inclusion of, 32–35,
    137
  giving yourself the gift of
    time, 64–65
  quiet time, 147–148
  resources, 50

revitalizing hour each day,
  38–40
traumas, dealing with life's little,
  189–194
travel, 69–70
Twain, Mark, 90

unconditional love, 3

volunteering for a charitable
  cause, 70

Waldman, Jackie, 126–127
Web sites, recommended, 212
weight issues, 169–172, 187
Weight Watchers, 9, 92, 208
  healthy weight ranges pro-
    vided by, 172
  maintenance, 102
  physical activity, 14
  program changes, 11, 14
work, finding fulfilling. *See* hap-
    piness, pursuit of
worry management, 140–143,
  191
WW Group, The, 14–15